BRAD & SHERRY STEIGER

Mystical Legends of the Shamans

INNER LIGHT PUBLICATIONS

Editorial & Art Direction:
Timothy Green Beckley
Typography by:
Cross-Country Consultants

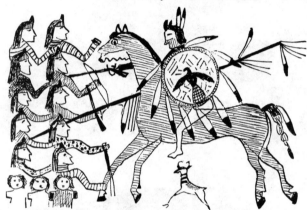

For foreign and reprint rights, contact:
Rights Department,
Inner Light Publications
P.O. Box 753, New Brunswick, N.J. 08903

ISBN: 0-938294-54-7

CONTENTS

AUTHORS' NOTE: Many of the Indian myths and legends that we have adapted, edited, and retold in this present volume were first gathered from numerous and diverse sources in 1884 by a remarkable woman named Ellen R. Emerson. We owe a spiritual debt to this early collector of Indian wisdom.

• • •

The publisher is indebted to artist Timoteo Ikoshy Montoya (Box 439, Hornbrook, Calif. 96044) for his excellent cover art titled "In God We Trust."

Born in Corpus Christi, Texas, 1956, Ikoshy is of Mexican, Mescalero Apache descent. His strong interest in indigenous culture has created a life-long dedication to the preservation and renewal of Native American Indian traditions.

Introduction

For those who were previously unaware of the power of myth and legend in conveying universal truths and teachings, the PBS specials featuring Bill Moyers interviewing Dr. Joseph Campbell, the eminent scholar of myth, became the most popular television programming of 1989. Now available on videotape, the examinations of the remarkable ways in which myths and legends are able to convey deep moral lessons through the technique of storytelling remain among the most popular of all documentary series.

In this book we present a collection of American Indian legends that have been repeated by generations of shamans who have employed the oral tradition of telling enchanting tales around the evening campfires. The incredible power of these legends remain undimmed by the passage of time, and their applications of vital truths for modern men and women became increasingly self-evident.

The campfire was the center of Indian social life. In most tribes, the women usually sat on one side of the fire and the men on the other. The elderly men gathered to speak wistfully of the days on the hunt when their arms could bend the bow with greater power and send the arrows farther. Warriors told of their adventures encountering tribal enemies. Young people swapped shy glances that initiated courtship. And the children learned the traditions, moral values, and cosmology of their people from their elders and from the shamans, the Medicine men and women.

Tuscarora chief Elias Johnson once commented how a vital part of Indian life was the gathering around the fireside. Here, he said, were recounted the historical traditions, the stories of war and hunting, and fairy tales handed down unchanged for generations. The warrior's enthusiasm for courage was kindled by such legends, and the small child was inspired to dream of future personal glories.

Chief Elias goes on to make an interesting observation which readers of this book must heed: It is very difficult for a stranger to rightly understand the morals of the Indians' stories, though it is understood by those who know them best that each tale is always an illustration of some moral principle.

The Native American people are quick to offer rites of hospitality to strangers, but they do not easily open their hearts. For so long has the Indian storyteller been ridiculed for his beliefs and for his legends by the pale face scoffer or scholar that the medicine people will not easily release the humor or the pathos of their ancient myths. The secret pathways of the Indian psyche are not readily surrendered to the casual or the indifferent.

It is for this reason that many readers may not fully comprehend or appreciate certain of these legends at first reading. These are not Aesop's fables or nursery tales with an obvious "moral to the story." In some instances, the reader may have to invest some effort toward understanding a culture or a tradition quite dissimilar to his or her own. The reader may have to drop his centuries-old acculturated judgments of "primitive people" and learn to read with his or her heart, rather than the brain.

The traditional Indian hears a thousand voices of nature that are mute to the average Anglo, but which are charged with life and power to the spirit attuned to the Earth Mother. There are an indeterminate number of images, suggestions, and associations which occur to a traditional Indian that can strike no chord of reverberation in the conscious or unconscious of those reared in other cultures.

With that understanding and challenge in mind, we beseech you to avoid a superfi-cial reading of these legends. Permit yourself to enter the silence within your heart that is open to expanding your awareness and your perceptions of the immense stretch of the spiritual and physical universe. If you are prepared to make both an intellectual and emotional investment in these legends, then we can promise you an enrichment in your own quest that will bring unceasing rewards.

Brad Steiger
Sherry Hansen Steiger
Paradise Valley, Arizona

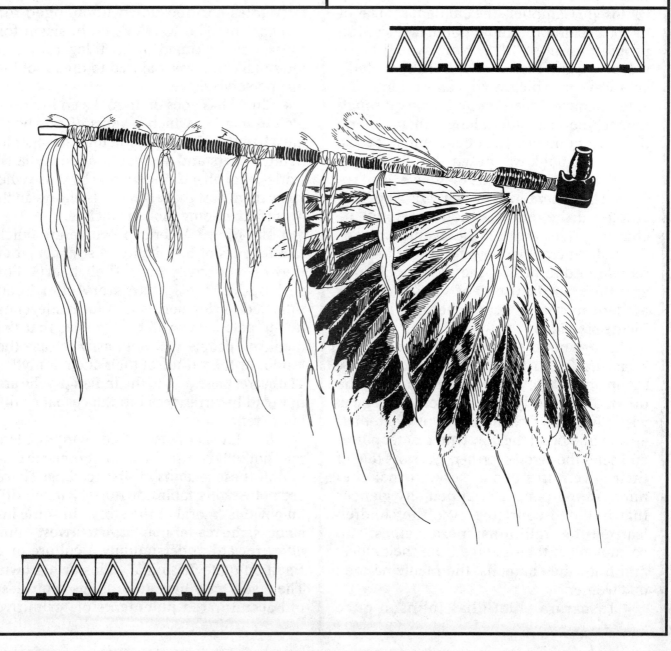

The Great Mystery

The traditional Indian did not believe in one Great Spirit as most Indians of the white man's novels, motion pictures, and television products would have us understand. The Indian believed that the world and everything in it was alive and had within it a soul or a spirit.

Most of the tribes believed that the world was permeated by a force, an energy, of magical power that was possessed by every spirit and could be attained by disciplined and aware human beings. It was the control of this force that could make the warrior impervious to the weapons of his enemies and enable the Medicine healer to drive out illness from the afflicted.

Although each tribe had its own name for this all-pervasive and mysterious power, the most commonly known are the Alonguin term *Manitou* and the Sioux expression *Wakan Tanka*. It was the early missionaries who confused the concept of a pervading force with their own Judeo-Christian idea of God and who named this energy the Great Spirit.

Dallas Chief Eagle, a descendant of the great Red Cloud of the Teton Sioux [Lakota]; once said that the Lakota never had a single symbol for the Great Spirit, the Great Mystery, because "...the Indian never sat around trying to figure out what the Great Spirit looked like."

Wakan, a word some authorities often cite as the "name" of the Great Spirit, is, according to the Lakota and Dakota people, better translated as "holy, sacred."

"We pay homage to this Great Spirit—or Great Mystery—through his creations—the Sun, the Earth, the wind, the thunder, the lightning," Chief Eagle explained.

Attempting a rigid definition of Medicine Power concepts or a simple explanation of the Indian's understanding of the Great Mystery most often meets with rebuke among the serious Medicine practitioners.

"Dogmas!" Chief Eagle scowled. "Who dares create dogmas? The Great Mystery sets forth guidelines. It is an insult to the Great Mystery to discard its messages in favor of following a human's created dogma."

The Great Mystery made nature for humankind to use and to preserve. "But nature also imposes obligations upon us," he continued. "We are only passing through life on our way to the Spirit World of our ancestors."

According to Winnebago tradition, in ancient days the Great Spirit awakened from a long dream, and finding himself alone, removed a piece of his body near his heart, mixed it with a bit of earth, and from them fashioned a spirit entity. Pleased with this creation, the Great Spirit gave expression to three other spirit entities in the same form. The first created beings became the spirits of the four winds.

After the Great Spirit had enjoyed the company of these entities for a time, He decided to create a female spirit being, who was the Earth Mother. She was first without covering, with no trees, no grass. Perceiving this, the Great Spirit created a vast quantity of grasses, trees, and herbs.

After this task had been completed, the Great Spirit noticed that the Earth Mother had grown irregular in her motions. He was thus obliged to create four beasts and four serpents and place them under her for support. This addition excited the four winds, who blew upon the Earth Mother so furiously that she rolled about more than ever. Seizing at last upon the final solution, the Great Spirit created a buffalo and placed it beneath the Earth Mother, thus balancing her motions and establishing harmony.

The Algonquin and various other tribes relate a similar account of creation, but it is upon the back of a great tortoise that the Earth Mother achieves her stability. Such a legend may account for the Turtle Clan being the peacemakers among the majority of Eastern forest tribes.

The most common term for the essence of the earth spirit among the various tribes was Great or Grand Mother—which has evolved into the currently popular Earth Mother—and the most frequent emblem associated with her was the tortoise. Cross-culturally, the ancient Chinese regarded the tortoise as one of four supernatural animals that presided over the destinies of the Empire. (The three others were the stag [guardian of literature], the Phoenix [guardian of virtue], and the dragon [guardian of national authority].)

The tortoise was also sacred to the Greek God Hermes. In the sacred books of the Hindus, Vishnu, in the form of a tortoise, is represented as bearing up the earth in the abyss of waters.

From the Chippewa— In the Beginning

At an unknown period a great Spirit Being visited the earth, and, becoming enamored with the Dawn Maiden, made her his wife. From this union were born four sons and in ushering them into the world the mother died. The first son was Manabozho, who is the friend of the human race. The second, Chibiabos, who has the care of the dead and presides over the Country of Souls. The third was Wabassa, who immediately fled to the north, where he was transformed into a rabbit, and under that guise became a powerful spirit. The fourth was Chokanipok, or the Man of Flint, or Firestone.

Manabozho was very valiant, and his first effort was made against Chokanipok, to whom he attributed the death of his mother. The war between the two brothers was frightful and long-continued. Signs of their battles exist until the present day.

In one of these combats, Manabozho cut huge fragments from the body of Chokanipok, which were transformed into stones. These stones, called flintstones, are to be seen scattered all over the earth, and are useful in supplying fire to the children of men. In a final battle Chokanipok was slain by Manabozho, who tore out the bowels of his conquered foe, and changed them to long twining vines.

After this signal victory Manabozho traversed the earth, carrying with him all arts and improvements, which he distributed among men. He gave them lances and arrow-points, and all implements of bone and stone; and he taught them how to make axes and the art of making snares and traps, by which they might catch fish and birds. During his journey upon the earth he killed those ancient monsters whose bones are now found under the earth; and he cleared the streams of many of the obstructions which the Evil Spirit had placed there.

He also placed four good spirits at the four cardinal points, to which is turned the pipe before smoking in the sacred feasts. The spirit that he placed in the North gives snow and ice to enable man to pursue game. The Spirit of the South gives melons, maize, and tobacco. The Spirit of the West gives rain; and the Spirit of the East, light. Thunder is the voice of the spirits, and to them is offered the incense of tobacco.

Manabozho now resides upon an immense piece of ice in the Northern Ocean. If he were driven off from the earth, it would take fire by his footprints, and the end of the

8

world would come; for it is he who directs the sun of his daily walks around the earth.

The Winnebago Account of—
The Origin of Humankind

Having created the earth and the grass and the trees, the Great Mystery took a piece out of his heart, near which had been taken the earth, and formed the fragment into a man. The woman then was made, but only a bit of flesh sufficed for her.

To the man was given the tobacco seed, that thrown upon the fire, it might propitiate the messenger spirits to convey prayers or supplications. To the woman, a seed of every kind of grain was given and to her were indicated the roots and herbs for medicine.

Now the Great Mystery commanded the two to look down; and they looked down, when lo! there stood a child between them. Enjoining the pair to take care of all the children which they might obtain in the future, he created the male and female the first parents of all tribes upon the earth.

He then informed them, in the language of the Winnebagos, that they should live in the center of the earth. The Spirit afterward created the beasts and birds for the use of all humankind, but the tobacco and fire were given to the Winnebagos.

How the Great Mystery Changed
Cranes into Humans

The Great Mystery created two cranes, a male and a female, in the upper world, and having let them through an opening in the sky, directed them to seek a habitation for themselves upon the earth. They were told, when they had found a place which suited them, to fold their wings close to their bodies as they alighted upon the chosen spot, then they should be immediately transformed into a man and woman.

The pair flew down to the earth and spent a long time visiting different climes. They went over the prairies and tasted of the buffalo, which they found to be good, but they also came to the conclusion that this food would not last. They traversed the great forests and tasted the flesh of the elk, the deer, the beaver, and of many other animals, all of which they found to be excellent; but they feared the supply of food from these sources would also fail.

After making the circuit of the Great Lakes and tasting the various kinds of fish with which their waters were supplied, they came at last to the rapids at the outlet of Lake Superior, where they found fish in great abundance making their way through its noisy waters. They discovered that the fish could be taken with ease and that the supply was inexhaustible.

"Here," they said to each other, "is food forever. Here we will make our homes."

Near the site of Fort Brady, upon a little knoll by the foot of the Rapids of the St. Mary, the cranes alighted, folding their wings as directed. The Great Mystery immediately changed them into a man and woman, who became the first parents and the progenitors of the Crane clan of the Chippewa.

The Great Spirit of Canadaigua Lake

Upon the level brow of Nandowago Hill, that looks down upon the beautiful waters of Canandaigua, there dwelt for many years the founders of the Seneca nation. No hostile tribe disturbed their quiet pursuits, and in peace the years passed by, while their families rapidly increased in numbers, and prosperity seemed to attend all their walks in life.

One day some children found and brought within the precincts of the village a serpent, which was very small, very beautiful, and apparently harmless. Loved by the young and cherished by the old, the serpent remained and grew so rapidly that the boys were unable to furnish it sufficient food; and the hunters of the tribe, day by day, gave it some portion of the results of their chase. Thus kindly cared for, the serpent soon became very strong and roamed about the forest or plunged into the lake in quest of its own food. Finally, it so thrived as to become of such enormous length that it was able to encircle the entire hill.

Having attained this marvellous size, it began to manifest an irascible and wicked disposition so frequently that the people began to feel alarmed for their personal safety. At length, oppressed with fear that if it did not actually consume them, it would, by its monstrous consumption of game, soon reduce the tribe to starvation, it was resolved in deliberate council that the serpent must die.

The early morning of the day following the council was fixed upon for its destruction. When the day dawned, the frightened people found the monstrous reptile stretching its full length around the hill, enclosing the whole town and blocking every avenue of escape. At the gate, the serpent reared its threatening head with jaws wide-open, ready to devour whoever approached.

Vigorously did the whole tribe attack it; but neither arrows nor spears could be made to penetrate its shining scales. Then some of the people, frightened and trembling, endeavored to escape by climbing over its body, but they were thrown back and crushed to death. Others frantically rushed to its very jaws with their weapons but these were instantly devoured.

Overwhelmed with terror, the remaining people retreated, and did not renew the attack until hunger gave them courage for a desperate assault, in which all were swallowed up, except one woman and her two children who escaped into the forest while the monster, gorged by its unusual food, was asleep.

In the recesses of the woods, her place of concealment, the woman was instructed by a vision to make arrows of peculiar form, and she was taught how to use them effectually for the killing of the serpent. Thus equipped, she sought the sleeping foe and, drawing her bow, she sped an arrow straight to its heart.

Writhing in its death struggles, lashing the hill with its enormous tail, the serpent tore deep gullies in the earth. As it rolled down the hill, it broke huge trees as it fell into the lake. With frightful contortions the hissing snake plunged into the water. Then, after disgorging its human victims with a great convulsive shudder, it sank slowly from sight. Rejoicing at the death of the dreadful enemy, the woman hastened with her children to the banks of the Canasdesogo Lake, and from her children sprang the powerful Seneca nation.

How Wasbashas, the Snail, Became a Man

Upon the banks of the Missouri River there once lived a snail who was very happy, for he could find plenty of food, and he was never in want of anything that a snail could desire. At length, however, disaster reached him. The waters of the river overflowed its banks; and, although the little creature clung to a log with all his strength—hoping thereby to remain safe upon the shore—the rising flood carried both him and the log away, and they floated helplessly many days, until the waters subsided.

The poor snail was left upon a strange shore that was covered with the river's slime, where, as the sun arose, the heat was so intense that he was irrecoverably fixed in the mud. Oppressed with the heat and drought, and famishing for want of nourishment, in despair he resigned himself to his fate and prepared to die.

But suddenly new feelings arose, and a renewed vigor entered his frame. His shell burst open. His head gradually arose above the ground. His lower extremities assumed the character of feet and legs; arms extended from his sides, and their extremities divided into fingers; and thus, beneath the influence of the shining sun, he became a tall and noble-looking man.

For a while he was stupefied with the

change; he had no energy, no distinct thoughts; but by degrees his brain resumed its activity, and his memory induced him to travel back to his native shore. Naked and ignorant, almost perishing with hunger, he walked along. He saw beasts and birds enticing to the appetite; but since he did not know how to kill them, his hunger was left unappeased.

At last he became so weak that he lay himself down upon the ground in despair, thinking that he must die. He had not been lying thus very long, when he heard a voice calling him by name, "Wasbashas, Wasbashas!"

He looked up, and beheld the Great Mystery sitting upon a white rabbit. The eyes of the Spirit were like stars, and the hair of his head shone like the sun. Trembling from head to foot, Wasbashas bowed his head. He could not look upon him.

Again the voice spoke, in a mild tone, "Wasbashas, why art thou terrified?"

"I tremble," replied Wasbashas, "because I stand before him who raised me from the ground. I am faint; I have eaten nothing since I was left a little shell upon the shore."

The Great Mystery then lifted up his hands, displaying in them a bow and arrows. Telling Wasbashas to look at him, he put an arrow to the string of the bow and sent it into the air, striking a beautiful bird that dropped dead upon the ground.

As deer came in sight, he placed another arrow to the string and pierced it through and through.

"There," said the Great Mystery, "is your food. And the bow and arrow are your weapons."

The beneficent Being then instructed him how to remove the skin of the deer and prepare it for a garment.

"You are naked," said he, "and must be clothed; for although it is now warm, the skies will change, and bring rains and snow and cold winds."

Having said this, he also imparted the gift of fire and instructed Wasbashas how to roast the flesh of the deer and bird.

The Great Mystery then placed a collar of beautiful shells around his neck. "This," said he, "is your title of authority over all the beasts."

Having done this, the Great Mystery rose in the air and vanished from sight.

Wasbashas refreshed himself with the food and afterwards pursued his way to his native land. Having walked a long distance, he seated himself on the banks of a river and meditated on what had transpired, when a large beaver arose up from the channel and addressed him.

"Who art thou?" said the beaver, "that comest here to disturb my ancient reign?"

"I am a man," he replied. "I was once a creeping shell; but who art thou?"

"I am king of the nation of beavers," said the answer. "I lead my people up and down this stream. We are a busy people, and the river is my dominion."

"I must divide it with you," said Wasbashas; "the Great Mystery has placed me at the head of beasts and birds, fishes and fowls, and has provided me with the power of maintaining my rights." And then he exhibited the gifts of the Great Mystery, the bow and arrows and the wampum.

"Come, come," said the beaver in a modified tone. "I perceive we are brothers. Walk with me to my lodge and refresh yourself after your journey." So saying, he conducted Wasbashas, who had accepted the invitation with great cheerfulness, to a beautiful large village, where he was entertained in the chief's lodge, which was built in a cone shape. The floor was covered with pine mats, and it had a very delightful appearance to the eyes of Wasbashas.

After they had seated themselves, the chief bade his wife and daughter prepare for them the choicest food in their possession. Meanwhile he entertained his guest by informing him how they constructed their lodges. Chief Beaver described their manner of cutting down trees with their teeth and felling them across streams so as to dam up the water. He also instructed him in the method of finishing the dams with leaves and clay. With this wise conversation the chief beguiled the time, and also gained the respect of Wasbashas.

His wife and daughter now entered, bringing in fresh peeled poplar and willow and sassafras and elder-bark, which was the choicest food known to them. Of this Wasbashas made a semblance of tasting, while his entertainer devoured a large amount with great enjoyment.

The daughter of the chief now attracted the eyes of Wasbashas. Her modest deportment and cleanly attire, her careful attention to the commands of her father, heightened very much her charms, which in the estimation of the guest were very great. The longer Wasbashas gazed upon the maiden, the more deeply he was enamored, until at length he formed the resolution to seek her in marriage. With persuasive words, he spoke to the chief, begging him to allow his suit.

Chief Beaver gladly assented; and, as the daughter had formed a favorable opinion of the suitor, a marriage was consummated—but not without a feast, to which beavers and friendly animals were invited. From this union of the snail and beaver, the Osage tribe has its origin.

When the Animals Ruled on the Earth Mother

When the animals reigned on the Earth Mother, they were very fierce and bloodthirsty; and they killed all the human beings then living, except one small girl and her little brother, who lived in great seclusion.

The brother was of very small size, not having grown beyond the stature of an infant, but his sister was of the usual size of maidens. Being so much larger than he, she was obliged to perform all the labor necessary for their sustenance.

One winter day the young maiden informed her brother that she would leave him at home when she went out into the woods. Previously, she had taken him along, but fearing some accident might happen, she gave him a bow and a few arrows and told him to conceal himself until he saw a snowbird, which would come and pick the worms out of the new-cut wood she had placed nearby.

"When the bird appears," said she, "draw your bow and shoot it." And she left him.

The young lad obeyed her directions, but he was quite unsuccessful. The bird came, and he was unable to get a shot at it. His sister, on her return, told him not to be discouraged, and she gave him permission to try his skill again. Accordingly, on the next day, to his great joy, he succeeded in shooting a fine large bird, which he exultantly showed her on her return at nightfall.

"My sister," said he, "I wish you would take its skin off and stretch it, and when I have killed more birds I will have a coat made of the skins."

"But what shall we do with the body?" said his sister, for as yet men had not begun to live on animal food.

"Cut it in two," he answered, "and season our pottage with one half at a time." The boy was wise, although of little stature.

This was done, and the boy by perseverance succeeded in killing ten birds; and from their skins his sister made him a little coat.

"Sister," said he one day, "are we all alone in the world? Is there no one else living?"

"There may be some others living," answered his sister, "but they are terrible beings, and you must never go into their vicinity."

This inflamed the lad's curiosity, and he determined to explore the country to see if he could discover any one. After walking a long time and meeting no one, he became tired, and he lay down upon a knoll where the sun had melted the snow. There he fell fast asleep.

While he slept, the sun shone so hot upon him that it shrunk and drew up his bird-skin coat. When he awoke, he found that it bound him; and on examining it he discovered that it was ruined.

He flew into a great passion and upbraided the sun, vowing vengeance upon it. "Do not think you are too high," shouted he to the sun. "I shall revenge myself."

On returning home, he related his disaster to his sister with great lamentation. Refusing to eat, he lay down as one in a fast and remained in one position for ten days; and then turning over upon the other side, remained ten days more.

When he arose at last, he commanded his sister to make a snare for him, for he intended to catch the sun. She replied that she had nothing suitable for such a purpose; she had only a bit of deer's dried sinew with which she could make a noose. But he said that would not do. His sister then took some of the hair from her head and made a string; still, her brother complained, that would not answer.

Then she went out of the lodge, and, while alone, muttered words of frustration. These words being gathered, she twisted them into a tiny cord, which she carried to her brother.

The moment he saw the cord he was delighted, and began pulling it through his lips; and as fast as he drew it, it changed into a metal cord, which he wound around his body until he had a large quantity.

He then prepared himself and set out a little after midnight so that he might catch the sun when it awakened. He fixed his snare where the sun would first strike the land as it rose above the earth; and, ho! he caught the sun, so that it was held fast in the cord and did not rise.

Now the animals who ruled the Earth Mother were immediately put into a great commotion. They had no light, and their consternation grew so great that they called a council to debate upon the matter and to appoint someone to go to cut the cord. This was a very hazardous undertaking, as the rays of the sun would burn whoever came near their source.

At last, after much discussion, the dormouse undertook the work. The dormouse at that time was the largest animal in the world; she looked like a mountain when she stood up.

When she arrived at the place where the sun was ensnared, her back smoked with the intense heat and her hair was reduced to ashes. She persevered, however, in her efforts, and she gnawed the cord in two with her teeth, freeing the sun. At the same time, she was reduced to a very small size, and in truth has remained small ever since. To her is given the name of *Kug-e-been-gwa-kwa* or Blind Woman.

The Great Mystery Gives Certain Animals to be Food for Humans

When the Earth, which was found in the claws and in the mouth of the muskrat, began to expand itself upon the surface of the water, the Great Mystery sat, day by day, watching its enlargement. When he was no longer able to see the extent of it, he sent out a wolf and told him to run around the ground, and then return to him, so that he might thus know how large the Earth had become.

The wolf was absent only a short time and returned. After some time the Great Mystery sent him out a second time with similar directions, and he was gone two years.

Again, after this, he sent him out, and he returned no more. Then the Great Mystery gave his younger brothers, *Ne-she-mah*, the animals, each his peculiar food. He instructed those animals, which were to be food for men, that they should not resist, but permit themselves to be slain, as long as the method of killing was a merciful one.

How the Sun and Moon Came to Be and How the Prairie Wolf Scattered the Stars

According to the Navajo, it was in this manner the sun, moon, and stars were built and placed in the firmament:

At the beginning, when the people had all crept out of the opening in the cave in which they had previously dwelt, a council of wise men was held to discuss the propriety of introducing more light upon the Earth, which at that time was very small and was only lit by a twilight, like that seen just at the breaking of dawn.

Having deliberated some time, the wise men concluded to have a sun and moon and a variety of stars placed above the Earth. They first made the heavens for them to be placed in; then the old men of the Navajo commenced building a sun, which was done in a large house constructed for the purpose.

To the other tribes was confided the making of the moon and stars, which they soon accomplished.

Then the wise men decided to give the sun and moon to the guidance of the two mute flute players, who had figured with some importance as musicians in their former place of residence in the cave. It had been one of the flute players who had accidentally conceived the plan of leaving that place for their present more agreeable quarters.

These two men, who have carried the two heavenly bodies ever since, staggered at first with the weight; and the one who carried the sun nearly burned the Earth by bearing it too near before he had reached the opening in the mountain through which he was to pass during the night.

This misfortune, however, was prevented by the old men, who puffed the smoke of their pipes toward it and caused it to retire to a greater distance in the heavens. The old men have been obliged to do this four times since the Fluter has carried the sun in the heavens, for the Earth has grown very much larger than at the beginning; consequently, the sun would have to be removed or the Earth and all therein would perish in its heat.

After the sun and moon had taken their places, the people began to embroider the stars upon the heavens in beautiful and varied patterns and images. Bears and fishes and all varieties of animals were being drawn, when in rushed a prairie wolf, roughly exclaiming:

"What folly is this? Why are you making all this fuss to make a bit of embroider? Just stick the stars about the sky anywhere."

Suiting his action to his word, the villainous wolf scattered a large pile all over the heavens. Thus it is that there is such a confusion among the few images which the tasteful Navajo had so carefully placed.

Tibikgizis, the Sun of Night: An Allegory of the Sun and Moon

Knowing no one on Earth except Ackwin, her aged grandmother, the beautiful maiden Ozhisshenyon determined to seek some acquaintance suitable to her age. So she left her lodge and pursued her way across the country.

When she had gone a short distance upon her journey, she discovered, on the tenth day, a vacant lodge, which she entered. Here she found ten distinct places in which the former occupants of the lodge had rested, and she concluded that there were ten hunters to whom the lodge belonged. She had not been seated here long before her conclusions were verified by the entrance of ten brothers, followed by one younger.

These brothers gravely entered the lodge in the usual order, the oldest first and the youngest last, while the maiden sat shyly just inside the door. As the tenth brother, on looking about, saw the downcast and lovely face of the maiden, he approached, and, taking the gentle maiden's hand, led her to his place of rest, saying: "I have become tired of mending my moccasins; now I shall have some one to perform the task for me."

After a year had elapsed, Ozhisshenyon brought a little son into the world; but the boy died. The loss was too great for the hunter, who sickened and died very soon after.

The widow now married the youngest of the remaining brothers, who died childless. She then married the next, who also died without leaving an heir; and thus, in regular order, to the eleventh brother, who was aged, and whom it became necessary for her to marry.

But as love declined in proportion as the age of her successive husbands augmented, she married the last without affection. Grieving much for the loss of her first husband, and never having been reconciled to the death of her first-born, Ozhisshenyon resolved to flee from this, the last and aged partner.

The lodge in which she and her husband dwelt was built and ornamented after the manner of the Chippewas' medicine-lodge—the door of entrance being at the east, that of departure at the west. Taking up one of the stakes by the western door the unhappy wife, with her dog, entered a cavity that was in the earth under the stake, and disappeared from sight as the stake immediately resumed its former position. She then took a slow passage, occupying a whole day, from the place where she disappeared to the other side of the Earth, which is at the east, where she found an aged man fishing in the sea.

"My grandfather," cried the woman, "the spirit torments me."

But Manabozho, for it was he, replied not.

The woman again cried: "My grandfather, the spirit torments me!" repeating the words twice over in imploring tones.

Manabozho finally answered, as if in anger: "*Wâhè, wâhè!* You disturb me. You annoy me. There is no other spirit on Earth than myself. Depart this way!" and he signed

her to pass upwards in the air, and go towards the west. This Ozhisshenyon did in silent obedience.

Now when the husband, on finding his wife had disappeared, had sought a long time for her, he came to the west door of his lodge, and, discovering signs that the stake had been moved, concluded this to be the place of her disappearance, and wrenched it up with great violence when he entered the opening in pursuit.

On reaching the other side of the earth, he, also, found Manabozho sitting by the sea occupied in fishing, whom he accosted rudely: "Where is my wife; has she passed this way?"

The old man made no answer. The hunter cried very loudly: "Speak! tell me!"

"*Wâhè, wâhè!*" answered the old man.

The angry hunter began abusing him with coarse epithets until Manabozho reluctantly said: "You have no wife. A woman passed here and has gone to the west."

Immediately the eager husband rushed upon the track indicated, neither giving acknowledgment nor farewell to his informant, which excited the anger of the aged fisherman, and he pronounced a curse upon the rude hunter. "Go, go,' said he, "you will run after your wife as long as the Earth lasts, without ever overtaking her; and the nations who will one day be upon the Earth will call you Gizhigooke" (the Sun of Day).

But when the woman came round again to Manabozho, being grateful to him for aiding her in her flight from her husband, she told him to take her grandmother Ackwin, who was alone, for his wife. This Manabozho did, while, in acknowledgment, he named the woman Tibikgizis (the Sun of the Night).

The eleven brothers of the foregoing legend were representatives of the eleven months of the Indian year, a reckoning like the ancient Chaldean Zodiac which consisted only of *eleven* signs. Every month had a name expressive of the season.

March: the Green moon.

April: the moon of Plants.

May: the moon of Flowers.
June: the Hot moon.
July: the moon of the Deer.
August: the Sturgeon moon.
September: the Fruit moon.

October: the Traveling moon.
November: the Beaver moon.
December: the Hunting moon.
January: the Cold moon.
February: the Snowy moon.

The Earth Mother and Prophecy

In 1984, Sherry Hansen Steiger was one of the few outsiders (*i.e.* non-Hopi) to participate in a private kiva and kachina ceremony of the Hopi Elder Grandfather David on the second Mesa. She learned there of the "star people" teachings and of the very serious and important role the Hopis believe that they have held throughout time regarding the future of the Earth Mother and the fulfillment of prophecy.

The Four Worlds of the Hopi

In the Hopi myths of their people emerging from one world to another, we may have a poetic accounting of a people's cultural, intellectual, and spiritual evolution—or we may have exactly what the Hopis claim: the record of major high civilizations that rose and collapsed in prehistoric times. It matters little whether one calls these ancient civilizations Atlantis, Lemuria, or Mu, but the Hopi myths record that the human race has passed through three worlds which the great spirit Massau has been forced to terminate, to purify, to rebuild, because of the people's corruption and materialism.

Now, the Hopi believe, the Fourth World is coming to a close. Once again a Great Purification is needed, for humankind has once again failed to keep its covenant with the Great Spirit.

Before the Great Spirit hid himself from view, he impressed his teachings, and special instructions on stone tablets. When the Hopi reached this continent, the tablets were broken in half, and the Older Brother, whose skin has since turned white, took his share of the sacred writings. The Older Brother's return to rejoin the tablets will signal the advent of Purification Day.

The ancient prophecies state that the Great Purification will occur when people turn to material, rather than spiritual things; when evil ones set out to destroy the land and the life of the Hopi and other Indian people; when leaders of men turn to evil instead of the Great Spirit; when man has invented something which can fall upon the ground, boil everything within a great area, and turn the land to ashes where no grass will grow. Sadly, it would seem that each of these specifications has been fulfilled.

Hopi traditionalists are storing food and water for the coming Great Purification. They have been told that there will be a terrible famine sometime soon. Canned and dehydrated foods, seed, kerosene lamps, bottled water and water purification tablets are being put aside in carefully concealed caches.

The Hopi Strive to Tell the World of Future Events

Oswald White Bear Fredericks, a Hopi historian and traditionalist, once remarked to Brad Steiger that the Hopi were aware that many people considered their picture-craft to be nothing more than primitive doodling. "But centuries and centuries ago, the Hopi drew a jet airplane on a rock which depicted our people arriving from the birth place of our fathers. Yes, centuries ago, we had a picture-craft of a flying saucer."

Speaking of the future survival of the human species, White Bear was frank in his assessment: "The pollution of our atmosphere is the worst thing that humankind has done. This pollution will get into the soil and into the physical parts of people, as a whole race of humankind. Worse, not only will people's bodies be contaminated, but their spirits. The Hopi are trying their best to awaken all the nations of the world to this part of their prophecies."

The Mystery of the Older White Brother

One of the most misunderstood aspects of the Hopi prophecies is that of the coming of the "Older White Brother." White Bear explained that the prophecy did not refer to the modern white man: "We refer to the spiritual brother who has understanding of all kinds. He is not of human flesh at the moment, but he will come. Certain aggressive actions by nations who think of themselves as Great Powers will set in motion a certain event that will lead to the coming of the True White Brother."

When pressed for a more precise arrival time for the Older White Brother, the Hopi traditionalist said that he will arrive shortly after the close of the century.

The Mesquakie Also Foresee a Time of Great Cleansing

The Hopis are not alone in their anticipation of a Great Purification. Our friend Don Wanatee, a Mesquakie [Fox tribe] who has proudly maintained the old traditions, sees a great catastrophe happening soon to "rearrange things":

"Over a hundred years ago, the Mesquakie prophesied a box that would sit in the corner in which we would see things happening far away and hear people speaking who would not be there. They prophesied great trailways in the sky. They said the animals would be dying. They said when many species were becoming extinct, man would begin to see unusual things. There would be terrible floods and earthquakes. It would be as if the Earth were revolting against its inhumane treatment.

"I think the great catastrophe will possibly be a great fire of some type, and it will leave pockets of men and women who will begin to people the Earth again. This is what the prophets of the Mesquakie have seen."

Chief Eagle Explains the Earth Mother's Nervous System

Dallas Chief Eagle of the Teton Sioux once explained to Brad Steiger that from the point of view of Indian theology, there is no such thing as the end of the world: "There are upheavals, colossal upheavals, but no great end of the world."

Chief Eagle went on to comment that he looked upon the Earth Mother as his relative. "I don't think people realize that our Mother Earth has a nervous system, just like a human body. I don't believe our fair Earth Mother can take any more of the abuse that it has been forced to suffer by man. And when the nervous system of the planet is upset, it has to readjust itself, just like any other organism. The Earth Mother has to make its own adjustments and retain its balance. And when it does this, there will be catastrophes on its surface...and mere man is going to suffer!"

Peboan and Seegwun: A Chippewa Allegory of the Seasons

An old man was sitting alone in his lodge by the side of a frozen stream. It was the close of winter, and his fire was almost out. He appeared very old and very desolate. His locks were white with age, and he trembled in every joint. Day after day passed in solitude, and he heard nothing but the sounds of the tempest sweeping before it the new-fallen snow.

One day, as his fire was just dying, a

handsome young man approached and entered his dwelling. His cheeks were red with the blood of youth; his eyes sparkled with animation, and a smile played upon his lips. He walked with a light and quick step. His forehead was bound with a wreath of sweet grass in place of a warrior's head band, and he carried a bunch of flowers in his hand.

"Ah, my son!" said the old man. "I am happy to see you. Come in. Come, tell me of your adventures, and what strange lands you have been to see. Let us pass the night together. I will tell you of my exploits, and what I can perform. You shall do the same, and we will amuse ourselves."

He then drew from his sack a curiously wrought antique pipe, and, having filled it with tobacco, rendered mild by the admixture of certain leaves, handed it to his guest. When this ceremony was concluded, they began to speak.

"I blow my breath, and the streams stand still,' said the old man. "The water became stiff and hard as clear stone."

"I breathe," said the young man, "and flowers spring up all over the plains."

"I shake my locks," retorted the old man, "and snow covers the land. The leaves fall from the trees at my command, and my breath blows them away. The birds get up from the water and fly away to a distant land. The animals hide themselves from my breath, and the very ground becomes as hard as flint."

"I shake my ringlets," rejoined the young man, "and warm showers of soft rain fall upon the Earth, like the eyes of children glistening with delight. My voice recalls the birds; the warmth of my breath unlocks the streams; music fills the groves wherever I walk, and all nature rejoices."

At length the sun began to rise, and a gentle warmth came over the place. The tongue of the old man became silent. The robin and bluebird began to sing on the top of the lodge; the stream began to murmur by the door, and the fragrance of growing herbs and flowers came softly on the vernal breeze.

Daylight fully revealed to the young man the character of his entertainer. When he looked upon him, he had the icy visage of Peboan, Old Man Winter. Streams began to flow from his eyes. As the sun increased, he grew less and less in stature, and soon had melted completely away. Nothing remained on the place of his lodge-fire but the *misko-deed*—a small white flower, with a pink border, that is now always seen immediately after the disappearance of Peboan.

How Summer Came Upon the Earth

Because of the desire of his son, a fisherman who was a Spirit Being, called together a variety of animals in a council, which he held for the purpose of discovering some way by which the people of earth could have warm weather. After some deliberation it was determined to break through the canopy of the sky and so get more of the heat and warmth of heaven.

The first attempt to do this was made by the otter, who is the jester among the animals. He took the leap without consideration, grinning as if it were great sport; but his smiles were soon dispersed, as he fell headlong through the air down to the Earth, where he found himself so very much the worse for the attempt that he was scarcely able to rise.

The other animals of the council now followed. The beaver, the lynx, and badger, each in succession made the effort, but all without the desired result.

Finally, a wolf took a prodigious leap, by which he made such a dent in the sky that, through the help of the fisherman and two additional leaps, a place was broken, through which they were able to pass.

On gaining the inside the fisherman and wolf found themselves on a broad shining plain, where, scattered about here and there, were large and beautiful lodges. To these lodges the two directed their steps.

On approaching they were astonished to find them occupied by birds of the most beautiful plumage, which were imprisoned in *mocuks*, or cages, and which were singing songs of wonderful sweetness. The fisherman, remembering his little son, began to open cage after cage as he passed from lodge to lodge, so that the birds, Spring, Summer, and Autumn, might take flight through the opening in the sky and come down to the earth.

Now the Great Sky Beings were not far distant from their lodges, and when they saw the birds flying out they gave a great shout in their voices of thunder and rushed to their respective lodges. But Spring, Summer, and Autumn had flown from their imprisonment in the *mocuks*, and it was only Summer whom they were able to catch, just as she was making her exit through the opening. With one blow they dissevered her body, so that only a part descended to Earth; and this is the reason of her being sickly since her appearance here.

When the wolf heard the noise and confusion, he slipped down the opening and safely returned to his home. Not so the fisherman. Anxious to make sure of warm weather, he continued to break open the *mocuks*.

He was at last, however, obliged to take his departure; but the opening had been closed by the Great Sky Beings. When he perceived this, he ran with great speed across the plains of heaven in a northerly direction, closely pursued by the enraged Sky Beings. Arrows of fire were hurled at him from every direction, but he still remained unharmed; when suddenly one arrow lodged in the small of his back, the only vulnerable part of his body.

Soon feeling faint, he lay himself across that part of the sky where he was when wounded, and stretching his limbs, said: "I have performed the wish of my son, though it has cost me my life. But I die satisfied in the belief that I have done much good, not only for him, but for my fellow-beings. Hereafter I will be a sign to the inhabitants below for ages to come, who will venerate my name for having procured the varying seasons. They will now have from eight to ten moons without snow."

He was left thus, having expired after his farewell words; and he is now seen with the arrow in his back, lying upon the sky, and is called the Fisher's Stars.

How a Brave Warrior Defied the North Wind

Strong Elk lived alone in a solitary lodge in the coldest winter weather on the shores of a broad lake. Thick ice had formed over the water, and he had only provided himself with four logs of wood to keep his fire. But each of these would burn a month; and as there were but four cold months, they were sufficient to carry him through to spring.

Strong Elk was hardy and fearless, caring for no one. He would go out during the coldest days and seek for food where rushes grew through the ice, plucking them up, and diving through the openings in quest of fish. In this way he had plenty of food, while others were nearly famished; and he was often seen returning home with strings of fish when no one else was able to catch any on account of the severity of the weather.

This North Wind observed, and felt a little annoyed at such perseverance in defiance of the severest blast that he could send from the North. "Why, this is a wonderful man," said he. "He does not mind the cold, and he appears as happy and contented as if it were the month of June. I will try once more and see if he cannot be mastered." Thereupon he sent forth tenfold colder blasts and drifts of snow, so that it was nearly impossible to live in the open air.

Still the fire of Strong Elk did not go out. He wore but a single strip of leather around his body, and he was seen searching the shore for rushes with unflinching perseverance. What is more, his courage was always rewarded with the abundance of fish.

"I will go and visit him," said North Wind one day, as he saw Strong Elk dragging along a quantity of fish. And accordingly he went that very night to the door of the warrior's lodge.

Meantime Strong Elk had cooked his fish and finished his meal, and he was lying partly upon his side before the fire, singing his songs. And North Wind, listening, heard him. It was in this manner the warrior sang:—

Windy god, I know thy plan;
You are but my fellow-man.
Blow you may your coldest breeze,
Strong Elk you cannot freeze.
Sweep the strongest wind you can,
Strong Elk is still your man.
Heigh, for life! and ho, for bliss!
Who is so free as Strong Elk is?

The fisherman evidently knew that North Wind was listening close by the door; but he continued singing his songs, and affected utter indifference.

At length North Wind entered the lodge and took his seat opposite Strong Elk. But this had no effect upon him; for the warrior arose and stirred the fire, making it blaze up with great heat, repeating the while, "You are but my fellow-man."

Very soon the tears began to flow down North Wind's cheeks, for the heat was very oppressive to him. Presently he said to himself: "I cannot endure this; I must leave."

As he departed, he resolved to freeze up all the lakes, so that Strong Elk could get no more fish. Still, the warrior found means to pull up new roots and dive under the ice for fish as before.

At last North Wind was compelled to give up the contest. "He must be aided by some spirit being," said he; "I can neither freeze him nor starve him. I think he is a very wonderful being. I will let him alone."

Shawondasee, the Lazy Lover

Shawondasse is the spirit being that dwells in the south; and he is a rich, well-satisfied man, whose eyes are always directed to the north. In the autumn, when he sighs, the northern land is filled with warm and delightful air, and the golden Indian Summer springs forth from his short sleep to gladden the eyes with beauty as it breaks over sea and land.

Shawondasee, being the son of Kabeyun, the father the four winds, was of an affectionate nature; but his habits were indolent, and he was never successful in his wooings. One day, while gazing toward the north, he beheld a beautiful young woman, of a graceful and majestic form, standing upon the plains. Every morning for several days Shawondasee's eyes were greeted with this lovely vision.

There was nothing in the maiden's beauty that attracted his admiration so much as the bright yellow locks that adorned her head. Ever dilatory, however, he contented himself with simply gazing upon the fair maid.

At length he was astonished at a sudden change in her appearance: her head became completely enveloped in a white, fleecy crown.

"Alas!" said he, "my brother Kabibonokka, the North Wind, has been on the plains, and, enamored with her beauty, has put this crown upon her head."

He heaved a succession of warm and quick sighs and lo! the air was filled with light filaments of a silvery hue; and the object of his love and admiration vanished from his sight. The Prairie Dandelion, which was the maiden of his love, had lost, with the sighs from her lover, the crown of age—the winged seeds that he had mistaken as a bridal wreath from the hand of a rival.

The Origin of the Lone Lightning

Destitute of parents, sorrowful and forlorn, a little boy wandered into the woods; for he had escaped from his uncle, who had abused him by denying him food to eat at one time, and then obliging him to eat more than he wished, making him sick with surfeit.

The day had come to a close and hearing the wild beats roar within the forest, he climbed a high pine-tree, where he found safety, and soon fell asleep. In his dreams a person appeared to him from the upper sky, and said: "My poor little lad, I pity you; and your many sufferings have led me to visit you. Follow me."

Immediately he arose and followed him. Passing upwards in the air, at last they reached the sky, where he was presented with twelve arrows and the command to go and waylay the wicked spirit beings in the northern sky and shoot them.

The boy, obeying, went to the part of the sky to which he was directed, and at long intervals shot arrow after arrow at the spirit beings, of whom there were a large multitude. Ere long, he had expended eleven of his arrows in the vain attempt to kill them.

At the flight of each of the arrows, there was a long streak of light in the sky. Then all was clear again, not a spot or cloud could be seen. The twelfth arrow he had a long time, carefully watching an opportunity to bring down a wicked spirit being with it. He was troubled with his previous lack of success, which was caused by the entities being so cunning and transforming themselves in a moment into any shape they chose.

At length he slowly drew up the last arrow and hurled it, as he thought, into the very heart of the chief of the wicked spirit beings; but, in an instant, the entity became a rock, and into this rock the arrow sank deep and fast.

"Now," cried the voice of the enraged spirit being, "your gifts are all expended, and I will punish you for your audacity in lifting your bow to me." Then he transformed the boy into the *nozhik-awä-wä-sun,* or Lone Lightning, which we now see in the northern sky.

Brad Steiger shown being initiated into medicine lodge of the Wolf Clan, Seneca Tribe.

Stars—Guardians of the Night

The Indians of old regarded the movements of the stars and planets as entities regulated by their own indwelling power. They believed the larger stars had been appointed by the Great Mystery as guardians of the smaller ones. Clusters of stars were thought to be villages of Light Beings, and the constellations were believed to be council-gatherings of spirit entities.

It is interesting to note the universality of the belief in the stars as the residences of spiritual beings who have a connection with, and a mysterious relationship to, human souls. In the Egypt of Ramses the Great such a belief exercised a great influence over the cosmology of the people, who linked individual destinies to the motions of the stars. The priestcraft of that time prophesied the temperament, life, and death of newborn infants from the conjunction of the planets at the hour of birth. Some scholars suggest that the origin of astrology may be traced to this period of history.

The native peoples of New Zealand believe in star spirits, but they conceive of the entities as being human souls who once had mortal bodies and who once resided on the Earth Mother.

In the hieroglyphic writing of the ancient Egyptians it has been asserted that the symbol for "star" signified a guiding or ministering spirit, a belief that would have been very similar to that of the American Indian tribes, who felt specific guidance from Star Beings.

The Star That Loved Humankind

The old chieftain sat in his wigwam, quietly smoking his favorite pipe, when a crowd of Indian boys suddenly entered, and, with numerous offerings of tobacco, begged him to tell them a story.

There was once a time, he began, when this world was filled with happy people, when all the nations were as one, and the crimson tide of war had not begun to roll.

Plenty of game was in the forest and on the plains. None were in want, for a full supply was at hand.

Sickness was unknown.

The beasts of the field were tame. They came and went at the bidding of man.

One unending spring gave no place for winter with its cold blasts and its unhealthy chills. Every tree and bush yielded fruit.

Flowers carpeted the Earth. The air was laden with their fragrance and was alive with the songs of happy birds that flew from branch to branch. There were birds of more beautiful song and plumage than now.

It was at such a time when Earth was a paradise and humankind worthily its possessor, that the Indians were the lone inhabitants of the American wilderness. They numbered millions; and, living as nature designed them to live, enjoyed its many blessings.

Instead of amusements in close rooms, the sport of the field was theirs. At night they met on the wide green beneath the heavenly worlds—the *ah-nung-o-kah*. They watched the stars; they loved to gaze at them, for they believed them to be the residences of the good, who had been taken home by the Great Mystery.

One night they saw one star that shone brighter than all others. Its location was far away in the south, near a mountain peak. For many nights it was seen until it was doubted by many that the star was as far distant in the southern skies as it seemed to be.

This doubt led to an examination, which proved the star to be only a short distance away, near the tops of some trees. A number of warriors were selected to go to see what it was.

They went, and on their return said that the star appeared strange, somewhat like a bird.

A committee of the wise men were called to ponder the meaning of the mysterious star. They feared that it might be an omen of some disaster. Some thought it a precursor of good, others of evil; and some supposed it to be the star spoken of by their forefathers as the forerunner of a dreadful war.

One moon had nearly gone by, and yet the mystery remained unsolved.

One night a young warrior had a dream in which a beautiful maiden came and stood at his side and thus addressed him: "Young brave! Charmed with the land of my forefathers, its flowers, its birds, its rivers, its beautiful lakes, and its mountains clothed with green, I have left my sisters in yonder world to dwell among you. Young brave! Ask your wise and your great men where I can live and see the happy race continually. Ask them what form I shall assume in order to be loved."

Thus spoke the bright stranger until the young man awoke. On stepping out of his lodge he saw the star yet blazing in its accustomed place.

At early dawn, the chief's crier was sent around the camp to call every warrior to the council-lodge. When they had met, the young warrior related his dream.

The Council concluded that the star that had been seen in the south had fallen in love with humankind, and that it was desirous to dwell with them.

The next night five tall, noble-looking, adventurous braves were sent to welcome the stranger to Earth. They went and presented to it a pipe of peace, filled with sweet-scented herbs, and they rejoiced when it took it from them. As they returned to the village, the star with expanded wings followed, and hovered over their homes till the dawn of day.

Again the star came to the young man in a dream and desired to know where it should live and what form it should take.

The next day, the Council named places on the top of giant trees or in flowers. At length it was told to choose a place itself, and it did so.

At first it dwelt in the white rose of the mountains; but there it was so buried that it could not be seen. It went to the prairie; but it feared the hoof of the buffalo. It next sought the rocky cliff; but there it was so high that the children, whom it loved most, could not see it.

"I know where I shall live," said the bright fugitive. "I will live where I can see the gliding canoes of the race I most admire. Children shall be my playmates, and I will kiss their slumber by the side of cool lakes. The nation shall love me wherever I am."

These words having been said, she alighted on the waters, where she saw herself reflected. The next morning thousands of white flowers were seen on the surface of the lakes, and the Indians gave them this name, *wah-be-gwan-nee* (water lily).

This star had lived in the southern skies. Her brothers can be seen far off in the cold north, hunting the Great Bear; while her sisters watch her in the east and west.

Children, when you see the lily on the waters, take it in your hands and hold it to the skies, so that it may be happy on Earth just as its two sisters, the morning and evening stars, are happy in heaven.

Throughout Earth's history, nearly all cultures in their religion or mythology have expressed a connection with—or an origin from—the Stars. Likewise, many of the Amerindian people speak of having come from various stars; and the Navajo, the Hopi, and the Cherokee single out the Pleiades star cluster as their true home. A large number of the Star People, those men and women who have experienced an awareness that their physical or spiritual ancestors came to Earth from another planet or from another dimension, name the Pleiades as their otherworldly home.

A Cherokee physicist, who lives in Alabama, says that he not only has a recall of a past life in the Pleiades, but he is also able to fit his alien memories together with tribal legends that his people came from another world.

"We lived in domed cities with translucent walls. We could fly, communicate with animals, transport ourselves instantly to other parts of our world. I remember my city as a golden color—a place of great beauty and calm. I came with others from my planet to help Earth through its birth pains into an intergalactic community and oneness. We were members of the priestcraft in ancient Egypt; alchemists in the Middle Ages; scientists and clergy in the modern world."

Some years ago, a very well-educated Cherokee, who was a Medicine Priest to his tribe and a practicing medical doctor to the Anglo community, approached Brad Steiger and said: "I have made an extensive study of the origins of my people. I don't believe there is any doubt whatsoever that there are Indian people on the face of this Earth who did not originate on this planet. I tend to think that once the Hopi prophecies are carried out; and their revelations are made known, they will bear this out."

On August 9, 1970, the 109-year-old Hopi chief Dan Katchongva was quoted in the Prescott [Arizona] *Courier* as saying that the appearance of UFOs over the reservation were in fulfillment of the ancient prophecies: "A petroglyph near Mishongnovi on Second Mesa shows flying saucers and travel through space. The arrow on which the dome-shaped object rests, stands for travel through space. The Hopi maiden on the dome shape represents purity. Those Hopi who survive Purification Day will be taken to other planets. We, the faithful Hopi, have seen the ships and know they are true."

The Hopi named the Pleiades *Huhokan* ("Those who cling together"), and they, too, consider themselves to be direct descendants of the inhabitants of the Pleiades.

Several cultures throughout the world, including the Hopi and the Navajo, use star calendars to allow them to chart the seasons and special events. The system utilized was based on a 260-day, sacred round, or minor cycle; and a 365-day major cycle, which equalled a period between midnight culminations of the Pleiades. Any day calculated on these cycles could not repeat itself for 18,908 days or 52 years.

A Daughter of the Stars Descends to Take a Husband

A young hunter was leisurely passing across a wide prairie when he discovered a peculiar circle upon the ground near which he had been heedlessly walking. The circle appeared to be formed by an admirably beaten footpath, without any apparent trail or footmark leading to or from it. This aroused the hunter's curiosity; and, hoping to see what the marvellous path might reveal, he concealed himself within the grass, taking care to have a good view from his place of concealment.

While lying thus in wait, he heard the sound of distant music in the air. As it seemed to gradually approach, he looked upward and saw a little speck or cloud, about as large as his hand, in the extreme height of the heavens. Continuing to gaze at this little cloud, he found that it gradually lowered itself; when, after a little time it

26

came so near that instead of a cloud it showed itself to be a basket, woven of reeds in which sat twelve beautiful maidens, who had each a kind of drum, which she gracefully struck with her hands.

The basket now began to descend more rapidly, and finally came down to the ground exactly in the center of the magic circle he had noticed; and the instant it touched the ground the young maidens leaped out and began to dance in the circle, at the same time striking a shining ball at each step as they tripped lightly around.

The young hunter was entranced, and he was delighted when he saw the youngest turn around the side of the circle nearest him. He rushed forward, thinking to seize her; but the moment the maidens saw him, they all leaped back into the basket and were instantly withdrawn into the heavens.

The hunter stood looking upward until they had disappeared, and then began to bewail his misfortune. "Alas!" lamented he, "they are gone forever; I shall see them no more."

He returned to his lodge; but the vision still haunted him. Whatever formerly engaged his attention now ceased to delight him. The following night, even in his slumbers, he dreamed of celestial music. Bright visions of maidenly beauty danced about him, making fantastic circles, which he vainly tried to follow.

The next day he went back to the prairie, determined upon another effort to seize the maiden who had escaped him. To conceal his design, he changed his form into that of an opossum.

He had not waited long when he heard the same sweet music and saw the wicker car descend. The maidens began the same sportive dance as before, and their motions seemed even more graceful and fascinating.

He crept carefully toward the ring; but the instant the sisters saw him in his ugly disguise they were startled and sprang into the car.

When it had arisen a short distance, he heard the elder say: "Perhaps it is come to show us how the game is played by earthly beings."

"Oh no," the youngest replied. "Quick! let us ascend."

And then they all joined in a chant and rose through the air out of sight.

As night was approaching, the foiled hunter returned to his lodge.

On the following morning, however, he returned again to the magic circle. Finding an old stamp nearby, in which there were a number of mice, the thought suggested itself to him that they were so insignificant that their appearance would not create alarm among the maidens, and accordingly he assumed that shape after having moved the stump near the ring.

Soon the reed car appeared descending; and, as before, when it touched the ground, the maidens tripped lightly out and resumed their sport.

In the midst of their merriment, one of the sisters suddenly noticed the stump and cried: "See! That stump was not there before."

"Frightened, she ran to the car; but her sisters only smiled at her terror, and gathering around the stump, jestingly struck it. Out ran the mice, the hunter among the rest. When the maidens caught the little animals, they killed all but one—the disguised hunter —who slyly managed to be pursued by the youngest sister.

Now in the eagerness of pursuit this maiden caught a stick from the ground, and raising it, was about to strike the little beast, when lo! uprose the form of the hunter, who clasped his prize in his arms.

The other eleven, amazed and frightened, sprang to their reed basket and were instantly drawn up within the skies.

The happy hunter now exerted himself to assuage the terror of his beloved prize. Gently leading her toward his lodge, he recounted his adventures in the chase—dwelling at the same time, with many endearing words, upon the charms of life upon earth.

His incessant kindness so worked upon her delicate nature that she consented to become his bride.

Winter and summer passed joyously away to the happy hunter, when his happiness was increased by the addition of a beautiful boy to their lodge circle. The scenes of earth life, however, began to grow wearisome to his wife; for she was a daughter of the stars, and her heart was filled with longing to revisit her native home.

Concealing her wishes from her husband, while he was away in the chase, she constructed a wicker basket within the charmed circle, in which she placed some rarities and dainties that she thought would please her father, and then taking the boy in her arms seated herself therein. Raising her voice in song, the basket arose in the air. The melody was soon wafted to the ears of her husband, who instantly ran to the prairie.

Alas! He was too late. He lifted his voice, beseeching her to return, but all appeal was unavailing. The basket ascended with his beloved cargo and finally vanished from sight. The hunter's grief was inconsolable. He lowered his head to the ground and was speechless.

The seasons slowly changed from summer to autumn, and, winter to spring. The hunter continued to mourn the loss of his wife and son.

"Alas!" thought he, "if she had but left my son I could endure the separation with less sorrow."

In the meantime his wife would have forgotten, in her happiness, the life she had led with him, but for her son, who as he grew older besought her to return with him to his father.

One day his grandfather, perceiving the son's sadness, said to his daughter: "Go, my child, and take your son down to his father, and invite him to come up and dwell with us; but tell him to bring with him a specimen of each kind of bird and animal he kills in chase." In obedience she took the boy and descended.

The hunter, who was ever near the charmed ring, heard her voice as she descended, and soon recognized the forms of his beloved wife and son in a car. When they reached the earth he clasped them in his embrace in the joy of reunion.

When the Daughter of the Stars gave her husband her father's message, he commenced hunting with the greatest activity. Rapidly collecting a large variety of specimens of beautiful birds and curious animals—of which he only preserved a foot or tail or wing to identify the species—he soon accompanied his wife and son to the car, in which they arose and disappeared from sight.

Now when they reached the star, the home of his wife, the father-in-law, the Star Chief manifested great pleasure at their arrival. He made a grand feast, and when his people were all assembled he proclaimed that each might take his choice of the earthly gifts brought by the hunter—whereupon a great confusion immediately arose. Some chose a foot, some a wing, some a tail, some a claw. Those who selected tails and claws were immediately transformed into animals. The others assumed the forms of birds and flew away.

The hunter chose a white hawk's feather, which was his totem, as did his wife and son. In the form of that bird, he spread his wings and, followed by his wife and son, slowly descended to the earth.

Rolling Thunder Speaks of Amerindians and Ancient Civilizations

Sherry Hansen Steiger's long-term relationship with Rolling Thunder, the powerful Medicine Priest and acknowledged spokesperson for the Cherokee and Shoshone tribes, expanded her awareness of the Amerindian-Star People link even more.

Rolling Thunder has commented that certain scientists have said that those people who are called "Indians" migrated over the Bering Strait from Asia. Others try to say that the Indians are one of the "lost tribes of Israel." It is all conjecture, Rolling Thunder states, and it is not at all necessary. The Amerindians know their own history very well.

"Some of it was written and put away at the time, but we still know it," he said. "We were here when the Earth was young. It shook when you walked on it. That's how ancient we are on this land."

Many people are stunned to hear a traditional Medicine Priest such as Rolling Thunder speak about ancient civilizations, Atlantis, and UFOs, but the truth is that nearly all the North American tribes have a rich and varied history of interaction with the People from the Stars that is as extensive as fairy lore is among the natives of the British Isles.

The Amerindian's Awareness of Centuries of Interaction with Star Beings

Amerindians, for example, were aware of the "magic circles" left in the grass by the Star People, just as their British counterparts knew of the "fairy rings" left by the "wee folk," and just as the modern UFO investigator knows of the strange, scorched circles possibly left by extraterrestrial or multidimensional vehicles.

And just as there are legends in Great Britain and Europe which suggests that in certain instances the interaction between humankind and these other-worldly visitors became so intimate that progeny resulted, so there are Amerindians who believe that such blending frequently took place between their own kind and the Star Beings. As we have subsequently discovered from our own individual research among various Amerindian tribes, it would not have been at all remarkable for the early Native Americans to consider that strangers might visit them from the stars, for they adhered to the universal belief that describes the stars as the residences of spiritual beings who have a definite connection with, and a mysterious relationship to, human souls.

The Star People

Star People research began in the period of 1967 to '72 when during the course of his UFO investigation, Brad Steiger began to meet men and women who claimed to have memories of their "soul essences" having come to this planet from "somewhere else." The great majority of these people claimed to have had experiences with UFO beings or multidimensional intelligences since their earliest childhood. Almost without exception, they were of the conviction that they were to somehow serve as "helpers" and "guides" during the coming days of change and transition on the planet Earth.

Most of these sincere people were well aware of how a psychiatrist might interpret their "memories" and their mystical experiences, but in point of actual fact, a good number of them *were* psychiatrists, psychologists, and university professors. These men and women argued that they had both the wit and the wisdom to distinguish between fantasy and a personal truth that was somehow an integral element of their private cosmology.

Pursuing the subject of their unusual memories, Brad found that a great majority of these unique men and women had always had a feeling, a knowing, that their physical —or spiritual—ancestors had come to Earth from another planet or another dimension of being. At least an equal number of these individuals believed that they had experienced a prior lifetime on another world or another dimensional reality.

Philosopher Eric Hoffer echoed such sentiments when he mused that he had always felt that man was a total stranger to Earth: "I always placed with the fancy: maybe a contagion from outer space is the seed of man. Hence our preoccupation with heaven, with the sky, with the stars, the gods, somewhere out there in space. It is a kind of homing impulse. We are drawn to where we come from."

Buckminster Fuller often speculated along similar lines. "We will probably learn that Darwin was wrong and that man came to Earth from another planet," he once offered as a wry comment.

Memories of Crashing Starships and Planting Colonies

Many of those whom Brad interviewed in the late 1960s spoke of a "starship" that crashed and left survivors marooned on Earth. Some had painted colorful scenes from their soul memories of that fateful collision on an alien world. Others somehow remembered a starcraft that had come to this planet about 20,000 years ago on a mission to observe, to study, to blend with evolving *Homo sapiens*. It was their goal that their own seed would enrich the developing species and accelerate the time frame when their Earth cousins would begin to reach for the stars—their true cosmic home.

A Mission to Help Earthlings Evolve to Higher Awareness

Interestingly, far from fostering cosmic snobbery or aloofness, such inner-knowings had caused these people to recognize that they had a mission to help others to evolve and to assist the planet Earth to survive. Their starborn awareness had created a sense of responsibility rather than a false sense of superiority. Nor, they insisted, did the awareness that one is essentially "star seed" and a "stranger in a strange land" necessitate one's withdrawing from the cultural environment in which one finds oneself. Rather, they stoutly maintained, the star-

born would become activists, seeking justice, equal opportunities, and spiritual freedom for all.

The sense of oneness with the cosmos so often articulated by these "starseed" was similarly expressed by Teilhard de Chardin when he said, "No longer will man be able to see himself entirely unrelated to mankind, neither will he be able to see mankind unrelated to life, nor life unrelated to the Universe."

Amerindian Legends of Star Wives and Star Husbands

It was sometime in 1972 when Brad began to refer to these men and women as the Star People. He borrowed the term from the traditional Native Americans, who believe that the stars are the residences of spiritual beings who have a definite connection with, and a mysterious relationship to, human souls. The Chippewa especially have a rich tradition of an interaction with the "Star People," who even took of themselves human wives and husbands and produced children—some of whom stayed on the Earth Mother, others of whom left in the "singing shiny blankets," to live in the sky.

Establishing a Pattern Profile for the Star People

As early as 1967, Brad had begun to take note of certain commonly distinguishing physical and psychological characteristics that he might combine to form a pattern profile of the Star People.

For example, he found that nearly all the Star People appear to have eyes with an extremely compelling quality.

Although they come in a wide range of physical shapes and sizes, and from all ethnic groups, birth signs, all social strata, all occupations and professions, the Star People project great magnetism and personal charisma. Strangers are instantly attracted to them and pour out their life stories and most intimate secrets within minutes of meeting them.

They seem to be very sensitive to electricity and to any other type of electromagnetic field. Many Star People complain of vertigo when standing under neon lights. Others seem to interfere with television or radio reception if they sit too near a receiving set.

They have unusually sharp hearing. They generally avoid noisy crowds because they readily become "audio sponges" and soak up sound to a painful degree.

The majority of Star People have a lower than normal body temperature. For them, 98.6 can be a fever.

A high percentage have extra or transitional vertebrae. An equal number suffer undetermined pain in their necks. Nearly all Star People endure chronic sinusitis. An astonishing number have Rh negative blood type.

The Activating Incidents

Perhaps even more intriguing to Brad than the anomalous physical similarities that he found among the Star People were the commonality of experiences that he came to term the "activating incidents."

For example, at around the age of five, nearly all the Star People experienced a dramatic interaction with an angel, an elf, a holy figure, or an openly declared UFO intelligence. At about the age of eleven, the Star People suffered some traumatic event—a severe accident, the divorce of their parents, a serious illness, etc.—that caused them to withdraw from the company of their peers and to retreat within for a period of time.

Osseo and Oweenee

Osseo was the son of the Woman's Star, which stands in the west at the close of day,
who, when under the baleful influence of a small star—an enemy to the Star of Evening—became very old and decrepit. Among his acquaintances there was a very beautiful young woman, the youngest of ten sisters, who was called Oweenee.

This young woman, after having discarded many suitors, became enamored with Osseo, who, with great delight, took her for his wife. This marriage was the gossip of the nine remaining sisters, each of whom had a handsome young husband.

It was the time of a great feast, and the sisters and their husbands were walking together to the place of the feast, when the sisters began to jeer at Osseo for his extreme age. Finally Osseo, exasperated by their persecution, turned his eyes up towards the heavens, and, uttering a peculiar cry, said: *Sho wain ne me shin nosa!* ("Pity me, my father!")

"Poor old man," said one of the sisters, "he is talking to his father. What a pity it is that he would not fall and break his neck, then Oweenee could have a handsome young husband."

Presently they passed a large hollow log, lying with one end toward the path along which they were walking. Osseo, as he approached it, gave a loud shout and dashed into one end of the log and quickly came out of the other a beautiful young man. His wife, however, had as quickly been transformed into an old decrepit woman.

Osseo led the party with the light springy steps of a reindeer. It was now Osseo's turn to show how love was above the circumstance of physical beauty, and he treated his wife with all the delicacy of attention that before she had shown him. He continually addressed her as his Nenemoosha—his *sweetheart*—and carefully assisted her when the path grew difficult.

The time for the feast drew near, and the party entered the lodge prepared for the purpose. While the guests were partaking of the food of the feast, which was made in honor of the Evening, or Woman's Star, Osseo's mind seemed to be abstracted from the scene about him. He tasted very little of the food, and often looked at his Nenemoosha, his Oweenee, and then turned his eyes toward the heavens.

Erelong sounds were heard in the air. Osseo listened attentively when he heard a voice speaking these words: "Osseo, my son, I have seen your afflictions. I am come to call you away from a scene that is stained with blood and tears. The earth is full of sorrow. Giants and sorcerers, the enemies of mankind, walk abroad in it. Every night they are lifting their voices to the spirit of Evil, and every day they are busy in making mischief. You have been their victim, but shall be their victim no more. Your evil genius is overcome. Ascend, my son, ascend into the skies, and partake of the feast I have prepared for you in the Star, and bring with you those you love. Eat of the food before you. It is enchanted; it will endow you with immortality. Your bowels will be no longer wood; your kettles no longer earthen. The one shall become silver; the other, wampum. They shall shine like fire, and glisten like the most beautiful scarlet. Every female shall also change her state and looks. She shall put on the beauty of the starlight and become a shining bird of the air. She shall dance and not work, she shall sing and not cry.

"My beams," continued the voice, "shining on your lodge shall transform it into the lightness of the skies, and decorate it with the colors of the clouds. Come, Osseo, my son, it is the voice of the Spirit of the Star that calls you away to happiness and rest."

The words were intelligible to Osseo—but his companions thought them some far-off sounds of music or birds singing in the woods. Very soon, however, the lodge began to shake and tremble, and they felt it rising into the air. It was too late to escape; they were above the trees in an instant.

Osseo looked around him, and behold! the wooden dishes had become shells of scarlet, the poles of the lodge glittering wires of silver, and the bark that covered them gorgeous wings of insects. A moment more, and lo! his brothers and friends, his sisters and parents, were birds of various plumage. Some were jays; some partridges and pigeons; and others gay singing birds, who hopped about, displaying their glittering feathers and singing their songs.

But, alas! his Nenemoosha, his Oweenee, still retained her shape as an old woman, robed in her earthly garb. With a supplicating glance he looked upward, uttering his peculiar cry he had before made, and which gave him the victory at the hollow log. An instant, and his wife was restored to her former youth and beauty, and they found themselves in the Evening Star.

"My son," said the Spirit of the Star, "hang that cage of birds, which you have brought with you, at the door, and I will then converse with you."

Osseo obeyed, and afterwards, with his wife, entered the lodge, in which dwelt the Spirit of the Star. Here he was informed of the cause of his earthly afflictions—how an envious star of lesser magnitude, jealous of the power of the Star of Evening, and its having the guidance of the female world, had attempted to destroy him and his wife. He was warned not to let the light of this star's beams fall upon him, for that was the arrow the star used, by which he had transformed him and Oweenee into decrepit old persons.

Osseo and Oweenee now took up their abode within the Woman's Star; and, after a little time, Oweenee presented her husband with a son, who was the image of his father. After a few years had elapsed, the son became old enough to learn the art of using the bow and arrow, and for practice he was allowed to shoot at the birds in the cage that hung near the door. He soon became expert in this art, and the very first day he brought down a bird; but when he was about to pick it up, it became a beautiful young woman, with an arrow in her breast. It was one of his younger aunts.

The moment her blood fell upon the surface of that pure and spotless planet, the

Star of Evening, the charm that retained him there, was dissolved.

Swiftly falling through the air, he passed through the lower clouds, and suddenly dropped upon a high and lovely island on a large lake. But he was not left alone, for on looking up he saw all his aunts and uncles following him in the form of birds; and in mid-air was seen descending the silver lodge, wherein sat his father and mother. Its bits of bark, looking like so many insects' gilded wings, glowed and gleamed as it floated nearer and nearer, to at length rest on the highest cliff of the island, determining their residence by its locality.

All then resumed their natural shapes, diminished to the size of Puckwudjinnes [elves]. As a mark of homage to the Evening Star, they never fail, on pleasant evenings during the summer season, to join hands and dance upon the summit of the cliff. Here fishermen have often seen their beautiful lodge and heard their voices in the dance; and to the island whereon rests the lodge, they give the name *Mish-in-e-nok-inokong*.

American Indian Legends of the "Allegwi"

Were there truly "giants in the Earth" striding across the Americas in our prehistoric past, as well as "Star People"?

According to their oral tradition, the Delaware Indians once lived in the western United States. At some point in their history they migrated eastward as far as the Mississippi River, where they were joined by the Iroquois Confederacy. Both groups of people were seeking land better suited to their rather cultured way of life, and they continued together on their eastward trek.

Scouts who had been sent ahead of the tribes learned of a nation that inhabited the land east of the Mississippi who had built strong, walled cities. These people were known as the Talligewi and Allegwi, after whom the Allegheny River and Mountains are named. The Allegewi were much taller than either the Iroquois or the Delaware, and the scouts saw many giants walking among them.

When the two migrating tribes requested permission to pass through the land of the Allegewi, it was denied. Bitter fighting broke out, which continued for a number of years. Eventually, the superior numbers and determination of the allies prevailed, and the Allegewi fled to the west.

The Allegewi next appear in the legends of the Sioux, whose tradition tells of a confrontation with a people who were "great of stature, but very cowardly." The able and resourceful Sioux warriors exterminated the Allegewi when the giants sought to settle in what is now Minnesota.

Excavating Human Skeletons of "Enormous Size"

Is there any archaeological evidence to support these Indian legends and traditions?

Rising out of the prairies and meadows in Ohio, Minnesota, Iowa, and other states are the huge earthworks of the mysterious "moundbuilders." Scattered throughout the Midwest, the mounds were apparently raised by the same unknown people.

But do giant mounds indicate giant people?

Enormous weapons, including a copper axe weighing 38 pounds, have been found in certain of the mounds. However, outsized weapons, implements, and huge monuments are not proof of a giant race. They could be objects of art or structures inspired by religious commitment. The best proof of a race of giants in North America—or anywhere else—would be the discovery of the skeletons of such people.

Several years ago, two brothers living in Dresbach, Minnesota, decided to enlarge their brick business. To do so, they were forced to remove a number of large Indian mounds. In one of the huge earthenworks they removed the bones of "men over eight feet tall."

In La Crescent, not far from Dresbach, mound excavators reportedly found huge skillets and bones of "men of huge stature." Over in Chatfield, mounds were uncovered that revealed six skeletons of enormous size. Unusually large skeletons of seven people buried head down were discovered in Clearwater. The skulls of the latter excavation were said to have had receding foreheads and double rows of teeth.

Other discoveries in Minnesota included "men of more than ordinary size" in Moose Island Lake; a skeleton of "gigantic size" in Pine City; ten skeletons "of both sexes and of gigantic size" in Warren.

Could these huge skeletons of gigantic "Indians" been those of the last members of a once-proud and majestic prehistoric race? In historic times, their numbers severely reduced, their great walled cities destroyed, they may have seemed cowardly to more aggressive tribes such as the Sioux.

Throughout the Old Testament, the wandering Israelites encountered many areas peopled by giants, whom they slew upon "guidance" from god—and the strong sword arms of such warrior-leaders as Joshua and David. In early struggles for "lands of milk and honey," the nomadic tribes of the Middle East and the Americas might very well have massacred the last of a species of giants.

The New York Times [December 2, 1930] carried an item that told of the discovery of the remains of an apparent race of giants who once lived at Sayopa, Sonora, a mining town 300 miles south of the Mexican border. A mining engineer, J.E. Coker, said that laborers clearing ranchland near the Yazui River "dug into an old cemetery where bodies of men, averaging eight feet in height, were found buried tier by tier....

On February 14, 1936, *The New York Times* ran a piece datelined Managua, Nicaragua, which stated that the skeleton of a gigantic man, with the head missing, had been unearthed at El Boquin, on the Mico River, in the Chontales district: "The ribs are a yard long and four inches wide and the shin bone is too heavy for one man to carry. 'Chontalies' is an old Indian word, meaning 'wild man.'"

In that same year, on June 9, *The New York Times* published a story about the discovery of giant human skeletons with a Miami, Florida dateline. According to the account, three fishermen had found the skeletal remains of humans eight feet tall in the sand of an uninhabited little island off Southern Florida.

Commenting on a fragment of one of the skulls, E.M. Miller, a zoologist at the University of Miami, said the mandible was that of a man and was probably several hundred years old. The fishermen stated that the skulls were unusually thick, the jaws protruded, and the eye sockets were high in the head.

Witnessing a Sacred Seneca Ceremony from Long Ago

When the Bercels built their new home in Ebenezer, New York, they understood that the lot had originally been a part of the Seneca Indian Reservation. On the night of February 22, 1966, Carolyn Bercel went for a walk with her dog along the Cazenovia Creek. Seemingly from out of nowhere came the howl of a strange dog. Her own dog froze, his ears pricked, his tail high, his hackles rising.

Then on the creek bank, there appeared a tall pole decorated with cloth strips in vivid colors. As Carolyn watched in astonishment, a buckskin-clad Indian wearing a strange headdress began to strangle a beautiful white dog.

"After he had killed the dog, he wrapped its limp body in bright-colored strips of cloth," she said later. "Next he wound strands of wampum about the animal's broken neck. Dimly I discerned glowing campfires and throbbing drums, and the smell of tobacco smoke penetrated my nostrils."

Soon the scene faded, and Carolyn Bercel stood there shivering in the snow, her own dog whimpering, leaning fearfully against her leg. Later she learned that time had somehow turned backward and allowed her to witness the Seneca Indian's New Year Jubilee ceremony in which a pure white dog was sacrificed for the sins of the tribe. Her research indicated that the last time the ceremony had taken place on those grounds was in 1841, a date that she determined by searching the records of the reservation.

Camping with the Spanish Conquistadores from 1541

On a pleasant weekend in August, 1941, Leonard Hall and a number of friends were camping on the Upper Current River in the Ozarks. Sometime before dawn, Hall was awakened by the sound of strange voices.

Startled, he opened his eyes to see several figures moving around a roaring fire about 100 yards from his tent. As he looked about him, he was even more amazed to see that the clearing on the beach was ringed by a dozen campfires.

Most of the shadowy figures were easily recognizable as Indians, naked except for breech clouts. Hall heard the occasional stamp of a horse's hoof, the murmur of voices speaking in several alien tongues. Some of the speech patterns were recognizable as Spanish, and Hall blinked his eyes in wonderment as he noticed that a number of the men seated around the campfires wore the rusted armor of Spanish *conquistadores*.

Hall convinced himself that he was either having a wild dream or else he had suffered some kind of mental deterioration. In either event, he did not wish to awaken his companions and receive any kind of confirmation that night. He crawled back into his bedroll and managed to fall back asleep.

When he awoke the next morning, he found no trace of the phantom campers, and he did not bother to relate his bizarre "dream" to his friends. Nevertheless, he remained curious about his strange experience, and he decided to do a bit of research.

The "bit" of research became rather extensive, and it was not until many years later in 1956 that he gave his eerie story to the St. Louis *Post-Dispatch*. His studies had disclosed the fact that in August, 1541, bands of *conquistadores* under the leadership of De Soto and Coronado had actually been in the Ozark area of the Current River.

Could it have happened that exactly 400 years later, Hall and his friends had camped on the very ground where a party of gold-seeking Spaniards and their Indian guides had built their own campfires? If such a thing can be so, we may at this time in our amassing of scientific knowledge only wonder what undiscovered laws of physics or superphysics permitted Leonard Hall to perceive flames reflecting off tarnished armor four centuries after the initial stimulus response had been transmitted.

Once again, it is noteworthy that neither the Spaniards nor their Indian guides took any notice of Leonard Hall and his sleeping friends. Different dimensions of time may overlap, but never, it would seem, can their respective inhabitants interact.

Indian "Ghost Lights"

Writer-fisherman Bill Mack recounted his investigation of the mystery light of Bahie Kino, a Mexican Gulf of California resort, for the June 1970 issue of *Fate* magazine. He stated that his first introduction to the *luz peculiar* came when a strange bluish light came through the windows of his camper trailer and awakened him one night about 10:00 P.M.

The light appeared to be about 50 yards long, and Mack estimated that its luminosity extended about 25 feet in the air. "There it sat," he commented, "just a blob of blue light!"

While he was exploring the area thoroughly in an attempt to find a clue to the source of the mysterious light, he learned that the light had been seen often and for so long a time period that it had been greatly feared by the primitive Seri Indians who had inhabited the area. Mack also discovered that an informal research team from the University of Arizona had spent three days in the area, probing, digging, and testing with an assortment of instruments. Their unofficial conclusion was that the *luz peculiar* resulted from the ionization of the air which occurs only under specific atmospheric conditions. They could not explain, however, why the ghostlight appeared only in the one spot.

About a month later, on his third research trip to the area, Mack watched the light begin to glow about 11:00 P.M. on a quiet, sultry night. The ghostlight remained visible for nearly two hours that night, and Mack observed it carefully. He had reasoned that if the ionization theory was correct— and if the light only appeared in one area— then perhaps something large and metallic might be the collecting agent. There could even be a meteor just beneath the ground surface.

"Like everyone else's, my efforts were doomed to failure," Mack conceded. "Neither my compass nor my metal detector were affected in any way by the ghostly glow …Maybe the Seri Indians are right, and the light is a spirit. From what I've been able to figure out, they have just as much evidence as any of us other investigators."

There are numerous "spooklights" haunting the nooks and crannies, mountain peaks and green valleys of this planet. And so far, all attempts at scientific explanations for the source or origin of the authentic ghostlights have proven to be unsuccessful.

A notorious ghostlight is located in the tri-state area of Spooksville, where the corners of Missouri, Arkansas, and Oklahoma come together. Spooksville's ghostlight is so dependable that it is advertised as a tourist attraction, and it annually brings in hordes of curiosity seekers.

In appearance, the Spooksville ghostlight resembles a bright lantern. On many occasions the light dims before spectators, then bounces back in a brilliant blaze of light. Hundreds of firsthand encounters with the mysterious ghostlight are on record.

During World War II, the U.S. Corps of Engineers scoured the entire area, using the latest scientific equipment available. For weeks they explored caves, tested mineral deposits, and staked-out highway routes. They seemingly exhausted every possible explanation for the origin of the mystery lights. The engineers finally left, confounded.

In *Spooksville's Ghostlights*, a small pamphlet written and published by Bob Loftin, such accounts as the following two reports are included:

Lousie Graham said that a spooklight perched on the rear window of a schoolbus returning from a school carnival at Quapaw, Oklahoma. Every child in the bus was convinced that the spooklight was attempting to enter the vehicle, and they were all thoroughly frightened.

"The light was so bright," Ms. Graham said, "that it temporarily blinded the bus driver, and he had to stop the bus. Just as we stopped, the light went away."

Chester McMinn of Quapaw told of the night when he was plowing after dark because it was so intolerably hot during the day: "Seems the old spooklight felt real neighborly that night and decided to help me with my plowing. I couldn't see too well, and I guess the old spooklight sensed it, because he started hovering all over the field where I was plowing."

McMinn said that he appreciated the spooklight's neighborly concern until it suddenly darted in his direction. The farmer says that he "absolutely froze stiff" to his tractor until the light drifted out of sight.

The theorists have lined up three deep to solve the mystery of the Spooksville ghostlight. There are the expected folk legends of ghosts, goblins, and the restless spirits of long-dead Indians and the standard scientific explanations of reflected moonlight, hoaxes, and misinterpretations of natural phenomena.

The present spooklight area seems to focus on a dirt road some eleven miles southwest of Joplin, near the Missouri-Oklahoma line. The light, according to the thousands who have witnessed its appearance, is seen almost every night from a half-hour after sunset to a half-hour before sunrise. It varies in intensity and time of appearance, and sometimes breaks up into distinct pairs of lights.

One serious investigator found that the spooklight appeared most often to float just above the hills down the roadway to the west. At rare times it seemed to come toward the observer. Through a telescope, the investigator claimed to have perceived as many as four distinct pairs of lights, with pairs of red lights appearing slightly to the right of pairs of bright white lights. The red lights grew dimmer as the white lights became brighter.

Many researchers have believed that they have discovered the answer to the enigma of the spooklight when they have taken note that U.S. 66, running east and west from Commerce to Quapaw, Oklahoma, is in direct line with the spooklight road. Light from motor vehicles, they postulate, could be bent, or refracted, out of its normal path and could appear to be bouncing balls of fire on the dirt road twelve miles away. The phenomenon of the bright white lights appearing slightly to the left of the dimmer red lights would correspond with the natural movement of traffic on a highway.

Area residents have conceded that the scientific researchers have made an excellent case for the Spooksville light being caused by the refraction of the light produced by headlamps and taillights on U.S. 66 twelve miles away. The problem is, the spooklight has been seen in the area since 1903—and that was long before the motor vehicles streamed along Route 66.

In his position as Curator of the Spooks-ville Museum, L.W. Robertson was quoted as stating that he had no idea what the spooklight could be. "I've looked at it about as much as any living man," he said. "It is here for people to see for themselves. I accompanied the U.S. Army Engineers on the experiments to explain away the light in 1946. Maybe the old Indian and Civil War legends are just as plausible as the scientific theories."

The Power of the Winged Ones

The Chippewas had a tradition that in the time-before-Time-was a bird of supreme majesty descended to Earth, which was then only a vast globe of water. The bird's eyes were fire; its glance was lightning, and the motion of its wings rippled the air with thunder. When its talons touched the water, the Earth Mother arose from the deep, bringing with her all manner of animals.

Many other tribes have traditions that tell of birds as agents of creation, and the winged ones became objects of religious ceremony among many of the native peoples. The journal of an early Roman Catholic priest records that the first time the Amerindian members of his California mission saw the representation of a dove over the altar, they asked if it was the Christian's thunderbird.

Although the Holy Spirit is commonly portrayed as a descending dove, the eagle has also been used to depict the swift and mighty power of God. Hebrew tradition also utilizes the eagle, together with the bull and the lion, as emblems of the Divine Being.

An early European traveler among the Mandan Indians told of observing a religious ceremony that involved two white painted eagles that had been carved out of poplar wood. The images had their wings in an outstretched position and their bodies were raised five feet from the ground. On the inner side of each of the notched pieces of wood on which the eagles rested was the figure of a man with buffalo horns formed of white clay. The images of the eagles, together with a painted figure of a panther, were said to represent power supernatural mysteries, and the visitor stated that the presiding Medicine Priest offered sacrificial reverence to the forms.

In the sacred works of the Hindu, we learn of the great Garuda, a large, eagle-like bird, that is often spoken of as a companion to Lord Vishnu. In some representations, Vishnu is depicted as riding on the back of this giant winged one.

The Scandinavians revered a great eagle which dwelt upon the branches of the tree Yggdrasil, a symbol of universal nature. In many instances, the old Medicine Priests attached the plumage and the heads of hawks to their shoulders, turning the beaks inward as if in communication with them. Similar depictions of the heads of hawks may be seen in certain pictures of the Norse god Odin.

Among some tribes there was a tradition of placing three long tail feathers from a hawk on each side of a Medicine Priest who claimed prophetic abilities. If the priest was too often in error or was considered of a negative disposition, he was allowed to wear only three feathers on one side of his head, thus becoming known as a "One-sided Priest."

Among the Iowa tribe, there was a species of hawk that was considered to be so sacred that it was killed only to obtain select portions of its body for the most powerful of medicines. This particular hawk was thought to inhabit only the highest cliffs of the most intimidating mountains and could only be obtained with the utmost difficulty.

The Iowas also believed that the hawk had the supernatural faculty of remaining for a long time on the wing. Those who stalked the winged one and were successful in bringing back its sacred body for medicine stated that they had seen the hawk fly away toward the Land of the Blessed.

Some tribes maintained that even more that bearing omens, certain birds might actually be spirit beings who had clothed themselves in the winged ones' forms. If a bird seemed to be flying with unusual rapidity of flight, a Medicine Priest might suspect a supernatural purpose.

The Linnet and Eagle

The origin of the Indian custom of using the feathers of the eagle for the decoration of their warriors is here given:

The birds met together one day to determine which could fly highest. Some flew up very swiftly, but soon became tired, and were passed by others of stronger wing. But the eagle flew beyond them all and was ready to claim the victory—when the grey linnet flew from the eagle's back, where it had perched unperceived, and being fresh and unexhausted succeeded in going the highest.

When the birds came down and met in council to award the prize, it was given to the eagle, because that bird had not only gone up nearer to the sun than the other large birds, but it had carried the linnet on its back. Hence the feathers of the eagle are esteemed the most honorable marks for the warrior, as it is not only considered the bravest bird, but also endowed with strength to soar the highest.

The Broken Wing

There were six young falcons living in a nest, all but one of whom was unable to fly, when it so happened that both the parent-birds were shot by hunters in one day. The young brood waited with impatience for their parents' return; but night came, and they were left without parents and without food.

Meeje-geeg-wona, or the gray-eagle, the eldest, and the only one whose feathers had become stout enough to enable him to leave the nest, assumed the duty of stilling their cries and providing them with food, in which he was very successful. After a short time had passed, however, by an unlucky mischance he broke one of his wings in pouncing upon a swan. This was the more unlucky because the season had arrived when they were soon to go off to a southern climate to pass the winter, and they were only waiting to become a little stouter for the journey.

Finding that he did not return, the young ones resolved to go in search of him. They soon found him, sorely wounded and unable to fly.

"Brothers," he said, "an accident has befallen me; but let not this prevent your going to a warmer climate. Winter is rapidly approaching, and you cannot remain here. It is better that I alone should die than for you to suffer miserably on my account."

"No, no!" they replied with one voice, "we will not forsake you. We will share your sufferings; we will abandon our journey, and take care of you, as you did of us before we were able to take care of ourselves. If the climate kills you, it shall kill us. Do you think we can so soon forget your brotherly care, which has surpassed a father's and even a mother's kindness? Whether you live or die, we will live or die with you."

After this resolution they sought out a hollow tree in which to winter and contrived to place their wounded nest-mate there; and before the rigors of winter set in, they had stored up food enough to carry themselves through its severities.

To make it last longer, two of the number went south, leaving the other three to watch over and protect the wounded bird. Meeje-geeg-wona in due time recovered from his wound; and now he repaid their kindness by giving them such advice and instruction in the art of hunting as his experience had qualified him to impart.

As spring advanced they began to venture out of their hiding-place, and soon were all successful in getting food to eke out their winter's stock, except the youngest, who was called *Peepi-geewi-zains,* or the pigeon-hawk, who being small and foolish, flying hither and yon, always came back without anything. At last the gray-eagle spoke to him, and demanded the cause of his ill luck.

"It is not because I am small or weak," said he, "that prevents my bringing home flesh as well as my brothers. I kill ducks and other birds every time I go out; but, just as I get to the woods, a large *ko-ko-ko-ho* [owl] robs me of my prey."

"Well, do not despair, brother," said Meeje-geeg-wona. "I now feel my strength perfectly recovered, and I will go out with you tomorrow."

Next day they went forth in company, the elder seating himself near the lake.

Peepi-geewi-zains started out, and soon pounced upon a duck. "Well done!" thought his brother; but just as the young bird was getting to land with his prize, up came a large white ko-ko-ko-ho from a tree, where he had been watching, and set claim to it.

But as he was about to wrestle it away, Mee-je-geeg-wona appeared, and fixing his talons in both sides of ko-ko-ko-ho flew home with him.

The little pigeon-hawk followed him closely and was happy to think he could show something of his talent at last. In his joy he flew in the ko-ko-ko-ho's face and endeavored to tear out his eyes, while he gave vent to his passion in abundance of reproachful terms.

"Softly," said the gray-eagle. "Do not be in such a passion nor exhibit so revengeful a disposition; for this will be a lesson to him not to tyrannize over any one who is weaker than himself."

With those generous sentiments, after giving him good advice, and telling him what kind of herbs to use for his wounds, he let the ko-ko-ko-ho depart.

While this was taking place, and before the liberated bird had yet got out of view, two visitors appeared at the hollow tree. They were the two nest-mates, who had just returned from the south after passing the winter there. Thus happily reunited, each chose a mate and flew off to the woods.

Spring now revisited the north. the cold winds had ceased, the ice had melted, the streams were open, and the forest began rapidly to put on its vernal hue.

"But it is vain," said the old man, who related this history, "it is in vain that spring returns, if we are not thankful to the Master of Life, who has preserved us through the winter; nor does that man answer the end for which he was made who does not show a kind and charitable feeling to all who are in want or sickness—especially to his kindred. These six birds only represent one of our northern families of children, who had been deprived of both their parents and the aid of their elder brother at the same time.

The Pigeon-Hawk and Tortoise

The pigeon-hawk bantered the tortoise for a race; but the tortoise declined it, unless he would consent to run several days' journal. To this proposition the hawk very quickly consented, and they immediately set out.

The tortoise thought that if he gained the victory it must be by great diligence; so he went along the earth, taking a straight line and allowing nothing by the way to hinder him.

The hawk, on the contrary, knowing that he could easily beat his competitor, kept carelessly flying this way and that way in his path in the air—stopping now to visit one and then another—until so much time had been lost that when he came in sight of the winning-point the tortoise had just come up and gained the goal.

The Origin of the Sacred Feast, the Medawa

Manabozho and Chibiabos lived on intimate terms in close retirement, for they were brothers and of superior powers of mind and body and were constantly engaged in planning for the good of humankind. One would have supposed that such employment would have received high praise from all created beings, but it was not so. There are spirits who are of an envious disposition. These jealous spirits inhabit almost every imaginable place upon the earth and are rife with conspiracies. Should any one be engaged in good work, he is interrupted through some mischievous prank performed by them.

Manabozho had warned his brother against the wicked machinations of the spirit beings and cautioned him not to separate himself from his side, as he was the more powerful of the two. But, notwithstanding his advice, Chibiabos ventured alone upon the ice of the Great Lake one day. As soon as he had reached the centre, the malicious spirits broke the ice and plunged him to the bottom, where they hid his body.

News of the disaster quickly reached Manabozho. He was inconsolable. He paced back and forth upon the shores of the lake, filling the air with his cries.

Then he began war upon the evil spirits and precipitated great numbers into the deepest abyss. He used all manner of means to torture them; and finally, weary with his labors, he sat down six years to lament, previously blackening his face in token of his grief. The whole country now was filled with the sound of his lamentations and his cries for Chibiabos, whose name he uttered in prolonged wails.

His inconsolable sorrow filled the repentant spirit beings with dread; and they consulted together, in order to find a way by which they might lessen it.

At last, the oldest and wisest of them, who had had no part in the death of Chibiabos, offered to undertake the task of reconciliation. He bade his fellow spirits to build a sacred lodge close to that of Manabozho and to prepare a sumptuous feast.

The spirits obeyed; and, taking a pipe filled with choice tobacco, they assembled in order, one behind the other, each carrying under his arm a sack formed of the skin of some favorite animal—as a beaver, an otter, or a lynx—filled with precious medicines culled from various plants. They approached Manabozho and invited him to their feast, with many pleasing words and ceremonies.

To their joy, Manabozho washed off his mourning color and then followed them. When they had reached the sacred lodge, the spirit beings politely offered him a liquor prepared from the choicest medicines, as at once a propitiation and an initiative rite, which Manabozho drank at a single swallow and his melancholy instantly departed.

The spirits began their songs and dances, united with various ceremonies: some shook their sack at him as a token of his skill; some exhibited the skins of birds filled with smaller birds, which, by some art, would hop out of the throat of the bag; and others showed curious tricks with their drums. All sang, all danced, all acted, with the utmost gravity and earnestness of gesture, but with perfect exactness of time, motion, and voice. Manabozho was cured. He ate, danced, sang, and smoked the sacred pipe. Thus, the mysteries of the grand feast, the Medawa, were first performed.

But to show more fully their repentance, the previously recreant spirits united their powers to bring the lamented Chibiabos to life. This they succeeded in doing; but it was forbidden that he should enter the sacred lodge, and they gave him through a chink in the wall a burning coal, and bade him go and preside over the Country of Souls. They also bade him make a fire with the coal, to light his kindred to that country; and this fire must never be extinguished, for all the future dead would have need of light in their pathway to the Country of Souls.

The Lover's Vision of the Happy Island

There was once a very beautiful Indian girl, more beautiful than all the maidens of her tribe, who died suddenly, on the eve of her marriage to a handsome young chief. Although her lover was brave, his heart could not bear his loss. He mourned as one without hope.

After her burial he sat near the spot where her remains were deposited, without speaking—musing and dreaming of her he had lost. War and hunting had no charms for him. He pushed aside his bows and arrows, for his heart was dead within him.

He had heard the old people say that there was a path that led to the Land of Souls, and he determined to follow it. With this resolution he left the remains of his beloved, and, after making some preparation for the journey, set out at an early hour of the morning.

At first he hardly knew which direction to take, for he was guided only by the tradition that he must go southward. For a while he could discover no change in the appearance of the country—forests, hills, valleys, and streams had the same familiar look that they wore around his native home.

There was snow upon the ground, however, when he set out; and it was sometimes seen clinging in thick mats upon the trees and bushes. At length it began to diminish, and finally, as he travelled swiftly along, totally disappeared, and the forest assumed a more cheerful appearance. The trees appeared to be putting forth their leaves, and suddenly, as if by enchantment, as he walked onward, he found himself surrounded by the budding flowers of spring.

The air seemed warm upon his cheek, while overhead, instead of wintry clouds, the sky was clear, and his ears were saluted with songs of birds.

The lover's heart beat quickly at these changes, for he knew he was in the right path, as appearances agreed with the traditions of his tribe. As he sped along, he discovered a footpath, which he followed. He was led through a dark grove, then up a long precipitous ridge, on the extreme summit of which he came to a lodge.

In the doorway of this lodge stood an old man, whose hair was white as snow, and whose eyes, though deeply sunken, had a wonderful brilliancy. He had a long robe of skins thrown loosely around his shoulders and a staff in his hand.

The young lover approached him and began to tell his story, when the old man interrupted him by saying: "I have expected you, and I had just risen to bid you welcome. She whom you seek passed here a few days since. Enter my lodge, for therein she rested, being fatigued, and I will answer all your inquiries, and give you direction for your journey from this point."

Having entered and rested within the lodge, according to the old man's invitation, the young lover, impatient of delay, soon issued forth from the lodge-door, accompanied by the venerable chief.

"You see yonder gulf," said the chief, "and the wide-stretching blue plains beyond. It is the Land of Souls. You stand upon its borders, and my lodge is its gate of entrance. But you cannot take your body along with you; leave it here with your bow and arrows, your bundle and your dog; you will find it safe on your return."

So saying, he turned and re-entered his lodge, and the freed traveller bounded forward as if his feet were winged.

He found, as he thus sped forward, that all things retained their natural colors and shapes, except that they seemed more beautiful—the colors being richer and shapes more comely. He would have thought that everything was the same as heretofore, had he not seen that the animals bounded across his path with the utmost freedom and confidence, and birds of beautiful plumage inhabited the groves and sported in the waters in fearless and undisturbed enjoyment.

As he passed on, he noticed that his passage was not impeded by trees or other objects—he appeared to walk directly through them. They were, in fact, but the souls of trees, and he then became aware that he was in the Land of Shadows.

When he had travelled some distance through this country, which continually became more and more attractive, he came to the banks of a broad lake, in the center of which was a beautiful island. Tied upon the shore of this lake he found a canoe of white, shining stone, within which were white paddles that seemed to be of the same shining material.

He immediately entered the canoe and took the paddles in his hands. Then, to his joy and surprise, on turning around, he discovered the object of his search—the young maiden—in another canoe exactly the counterpart of his. She, having imitated his motions in gathering up the paddles and making preparations for embarking, followed him as he pushed off from shore.

The waves of the lake soon began to rise, and, at a distance, looked ready to submerge them in their watery embrace; but yet, on approaching their white edges, they seemed to melt away. Still, as these enormous waves followed one another in quick succession, they kept the couple in continual fear; for they felt no certainty but that some one of them might break upon their canoes and bring them to destruction.

Added to this perpetual fear, the water of the lake was so clear that it disclosed to their affrighted gaze large heaps of bones of human beings who had perished before. And, as they moved on, they saw many persons struggling and sinking in the waves. Old men and women, and young men and maidens, were there; and but few were able to pass over. The children alone were seen to live on without fear.

However, notwithstanding their terror, the young man and maiden moved unharmed along, for their deeds in life had been free from evil, and the Master of Life had decreed their safety.

At length, they leaped out upon the shore of the Happy Island, the place of their destination, and wandered together over the blissful fields, where everything was formed to delight the eye and please the ear. The air itself was like food, and nourished and strengthened them. There were no tempests. No one shivered for the want of warm clothes. No one suffered from hunger. No one mourned for the dead. They saw no graves. They heard of no wars. There was no hunting of animals.

Gladly the young lover would have remained forever with his beloved in this beautiful land, but this was not permitted. Although he did not see the Master of Life, he heard his voice in a soft breeze which commanded his return: "Go back," said the voice, "to the land from whence you came. Your time has not yet come; your work is not finished, and the duties for which I made you are not completed. Return to your people and accomplish all the duties of a brave man. You will be the ruler of your tribe for many years. My messenger at the gate shall instruct you in your future work, when he surrenders your body. Listen to him, and you shall afterwards rejoin the spirit which you must now leave behind. She is accepted, and will dwell here forever, as young and as happy as when I called her from the Land of Snows."

And with this the Lover's Vision closed.

Sayadio, and the Magic Cup

Very sad was the heart of Sayadio, for his sister had departed to the Land of Souls, to the Isle of the Blessed. With his head covered and bent to the ground in the deepest dejection, he spent many hours in mournful reflection.

On a certain night, when thus meditating on his loss, Sayadio received awareness from his spirit guide that he was permitted to go to the Land of Souls and once more greet his beloved sister. He made preparations with haste and started on his journey, resolving to bring her back on his return.

His path was long and tedious. He had nearly given up his purpose in despair when he met an old man, who gave him a magic cup with which he might dip up the spirit of his sister, should he succeed in finding her; and he went on with a buoyant step. But when he had reached the Land of Souls he was astonished to find that the spirits all fled from him. As his sister was among them, he persisted in calling her name over and over again, although there was no response.

At this time, according to the custom of the isle, the inhabitants began to gather for a dance; and Ta-ren-ya-wa-go, the master of ceremonies, seeing the perplexity of the young man, kindly offered to aid him by furnishing him with a mystical rattle of great power. Very soon the deep-sounding *tawaie-gun*, or spirit-drum, was beaten for a choral dance, and Tarenyawago accompanied the drug with the music of the Indian flute.

The effect was instantaneous: the spirits commenced a strange and bewildering dance, in circles as vast as the spirit-land. Sayadio saw his sister among the dancers, and, making a sudden sweep with his cup, dipped up the entranced spirit, securely fastening her within; but this was in opposition to the efforts of the captivated soul.

Retracing his steps, Sayadio soon reached his lodge with his precious charge in perfect safety. His own and his sister's friends were immediately summoned, and the body of the maiden brought from its burial-place to be reanimated with its spirit.

Everything was ready for the ceremonies of the resurrection, when the thoughtless curiosity of one of his female friends frustrated all—she peeped into the magic cup and out flew the imprisoned soul! Consternation filled all hearts. The brother was called.

Overwhelmed with grief, he gazed frantically into the sky, calling upon the departed spirit to return; but there was no response. No sign of the one he had lost could be seen in its blue vault. Sayadio returned to his lodge in despair. Mourning in silence, he sought no more to recall his dead.

Adventures of a Warrior's Soul

In a great battle fought between two tribes of Indians, a warrior of eminence was wounded, and his companions thought he was dead. They placed his body in a sitting posture on the field of battle, his back being supported by a tree, his face turned towards the enemy's country. They placed on him his head-dress of feathers and leaned his bow against his shoulders. They then left him and returned to their homes.

The warrior, however, heard and saw all they did. Although his body was deprived of muscular motion, his soul was living within it. He heard them lament his death, and he felt their touch as they set him upright against the tree.

"They will not be so cruel as to leave me here," he thought to himself. "I am certainly not dead. I have the use of my senses."

His anguish was extreme when he saw them, one after another, depart—until he was left alone among the dead. He could not move a limb nor a muscle, and he felt as if he were buried in his own body.

Horrid agonies came over him. He exerted himself, but found that he had no power over his muscles.

At last he appeared to leap out of himself. He first stood up, then followed his friends.

He soon overtook them; but when he arrived at their camp, no one noticed him. He spoke to them, but no one answered. He seemed to be invisible to them, and his voice appeared to have no sound. Unconscious, however, of his body's being left behind, he thought their conduct most strange.

He determined to follow them, and exactly imitated all they did—walking when they walked, running when they ran, sleeping when they slept. But only unbroken silence was maintained as to his presence.

When evening came, he addressed the party. "Is it possible," said he, "that you do not see me, nor understand me? Will you permit me to starve when you have plenty? Is there no one who recollects me?"

With similar sentiments he continued to talk to them and to upbraid them at every stage of their homeward journey; but his words seemed to pass like the sounds of the wind. At length they reached the village, and the women and children and old men came out, according to custom, to welcome the returning war party. They set up the shout of praise: "*Kumandjing! Kumandjing! Kumandjing!* They have met, fought, and conquered!" was heard at every side. Group after group repeated the cry:

> "Kumandjing! Kumandjing!
>   Kumandjing!
> They have met, fought, and
>   conquered!"

The warrior's absence was soon noticed, but this did not mar the general joy. A thousand inquiries were made, and he heard his own fate described—how he fought bravely, was killed, and left among the dead.

"It is not true," replied the indignant warrior, "that I was killed and left among the dead upon the field of battle. I am here. I live, I move. See me!"

No one answered. He then walked to his lodge. He saw his wife tearing her hair and lamenting his fate. He asked her to bind up his wounds. She made no reply. He placed his mouth close to her ear and called for food. She did not notice it. He drew back his arm and struck her a blow. She felt nothing.

Thus foiled, he determined to go back. He followed the track of the warriors. It was four days' journey.

During three days he met with nothing extraordinary; but on the fourth, towards evening, as he drew near the skirts of the battlefield, he saw a fire in the path. He stepped on one side, but the fire also moved its position. He crossed to the other side, but the fire was still before him. Whichever way he took, the fire appeared and barred his approach.

At this moment he spied the enemy of his fortunes in the form of a Moccasin, or flat-headed snake. "My son," said the reptile, "you have heretofore been considered a brave man; but beware of this fire. It is a strong spirit. You must appease it by the sacred gift."

The warrior put his hand to his side; but he had left his sack behind him. "Evil Spirit!" he exclaimed, addressing the flame, "why do you bar my approach? Know that I am a spirit. I have never been defeated by my enemies; and I will not be defeated by you."

So saying. the warrior made a sudden effort and leaped through the flames. In this effort he awoke from his trance.

He had been eight days on the battlefield. He found himself sitting on the ground, with his back supported by a tree, and his bow leaning against his shoulder, as his friends had left him.

He looked up and beheld a large *ghee niew,* or war-eagle, sitting in the tree, which he immediately recognized as his guardian spirit and totem. The bird had watched his body and prevented other birds of prey from devouring it.

The warrior arose and stood a few moments, but found himself weak and emaciated. By the use of forest arts in which he was versed, he succeeded in returning home.

When he came near his village, he uttered the *sa-sa-kwan,* or war-cry, which threw the people into an uproar. But while they were debating the meaning of the unexpected sound, the wounded chief was ushered into their midst.

He related his adventures and concluded his narrative by telling them that it is pleasing to the spirits of the dead to have a fire lit upon the graves at night after their burial. He gave as a reason that it is four days' travel to the place appointed as the residence of the soul, and it requires a light every night at the place of its encampment. If the friends of the deceased neglect this rite, the spirit is compelled to build a fire for itself.

Moowis, the Snow-Image, and the Indian Coquette

There lived in a large Indian village a beautiful maiden who was greatly admired by all the warriors and hunters of the tribe. Among these warriors there was one young man who desired greatly to make this maiden his wife, but he had been rejected in an insulting manner; for she was a fearless coquette and acted according to her own pleasure, without regard to others.

She had, in reply to his attentions, placed her three fingers upon her thumb, and deliberately opened them in his face—which is an expression of the highest contempt—upon which he had retired from her presence in deep dejection. As the refusal was made in the presence of others, it was soon reported all over the village, to his great mortification.

This young man became very moody and taciturn, and finally took to his couch of skins. He would not leave it, even when the villagers prepared to break up camp and move off to the place of their summer residence.

But when they had completed their preparations and had left him solitary and alone, he arose; and after listening attentively until all were silent far and near, he then, with great animation, set himself to action, for he had resolved on a plan of revenge.

Calling upon his personal guiding spirit for assistance, he carefully gathered up all the soiled bits of cloth and fragments of finery, together with the cast off-clothing and ornaments that had been either forgotten or lost by the departed band. This motley collection he then carefully restored to its original beauty, piece by piece; and he made a part into coat and leggings, which he trimmed elaborately with beads. He also selected material for moccasins, which he garnished with beads.

Having done this, he searched for cast-out bones of animals, pieces of skins, bits of meat. He cemented them together with snow and dirt, and he pressed them firmly into the clothes that he had prepared. He fashioned them into the shape of a tall, handsome man, in whose hand he placed a bow and arrow, at the same time decorating his head with a frontlet of feathers.

Again calling upon his guiding spirit, he bade the image stand forth, breathing upon him the breath of life. The image stood forth a living man—a man made of rags and dirt.

"Moowis," said the young man, "follow me, and I will direct your actions henceforth."

The two walked straight forward to the summer encampment, where they were received with great attention by the whole band. Great was the admiration felt and expressed by the Indian maidens for Moowis, the handsome stranger; and chief among these admiring maidens was the belle who had so haughtily refused the young man.

Completely infatuated, she invited Moowis and her discarded lover to the lodge of her mother. There her hospitality would have soon put an end to the Snow-image's career by placing him nearest the fire, had he not adroitly contrived to take another seat—a move that at the same time saved him from melting and secured the grateful admiration of the belle, who considered his removal from the honored seat by the fire an indication of a magnanimous and hardy spirit.

Moowis, readily perceiving his accidental advantage, commenced a triumphant wooing; and the rejected young man—who accompanied him to the lodge with the secret hope that he belle might show some kindness toward himself—departed, leaving the successful lover to establish himself in the bridegroom's seat by the side of the maiden.

On the morning following the marriage, Moowis arose, adjusted his plumes, gathered up his bow and arrows. Turning to his wife, he said: "I must go, for I have important business to transact, and there are many hills and streams between me and the object of my journey."

"I will go with you," replied his bride.

"It is too far," he replied. "And you are little able to encounter the perils of the way."

"It is not so far but that I can go," she responded. "And there are no dangers that I will not fully share with you."

Moowis now went to the lodge of his master, the young man, and related to him the replies of his bride, so full of devotion. Pity for a moment entered the breast of the rejected lover.

"But it is her own folly," he said. "She has turned away from the counsels of prudence, and she must submit to her fate."

Then Moowis, the Snow-image, departed, followed by his wife at a distance, as was the custom. The way was rough and intricate, and she was unable to keep up with his rapid pace, although she struggled hard and perseveringly to do so.

Moowis had been long out of her sight when the sun arose and commenced the work of dissolution upon his snow-formed body. As he began to melt away, his misguided bride found piece after piece of his clothing in the path. His mittens, then his moccasins, his leggings and coat—each were found upon the ground in their original soiled condition. But still she followed, over rocks and across marshes, wherever she spotted a bit of his garments.

"Moowis! Moowis!" at last she cried; *"nin ge won e win ig; ne won e wig!"* ("you have led me astray; I have lost my way!")

But she received no reply; and, almost frantic with fear, she wandered through the woods, sometimes wildly leaping over a fallen tree or springing upon a high rock, still hoping to see her lost husband walking in the distance.

Day after day departed, and yet she walked on. Through the woods her voice could be heard calling, "Moowis! Moowis! *nin ge won e win ig!*"

There was no reply. The deluded wife wandered on for many months, until fatigue and exposure brought her to a lonely and unlamented death. And now, in the deep recesses of the wood, her unhappy voice is often heard repeating—"*Moo-wis! Moowis! nin ge won e win ig; ne won e wig!*"

The Gift of Corn—or, Mondamin, the Red Plume

Masswa was a famous magician, who inhabited the Manatoline Islands, in company with two young men. Among the many marvelous things accomplished by him, the following has excited the most wonder.

One day he arose early and started on a hunting excursion, leaving the young men asleep. Passing through a dense wood, he came unexpectedly to an open plain, very wide and extensive. He was directing his steps across the plain when he discovered a man of small stature, wearing a red feather on his head, who appeared suddenly before him, and accosted him with a familiar air, saying cheerfully, "Where are you going!" and, when answered, inviting him to smoke.

"Pray," said the little man while each puffed on his pipe, "wherein does your strength life?"

"My strength," answered Masswa, "is similar to that of the human race, and I am no stronger."

"We must wrestle," said Red Plume, the small man. "And if you should make me fall, you shall say to me, 'I have thrown you—*wa-ge-me-na.*'"

Laying aside their pipes, Red Plume and Masswaz and the magician commenced wrestling. For a long time the strife was doubtful. Red Plume, although very small, proved to be very active, and the magician sometimes grew faint in the struggle. At length, however, Red Plume was foiled, and was thrown to the ground.

"I have thrown you—*wa-ge-me-na*," cried Masswa. And in an instant his antagonist vanished from sight. On observing, however, the spot where he was thrown, the magician discovered a crooked ear of Indian corn—the Mondamin—lying on the ground, with the usual red hairy tassel at the top.

While he was wonderingly gazing at this mysterious sight, a voice from the Mondamin addressed him.

"Now," spake the voice "divest me of my covering; and when you find my body, separate it from the spine upon which it grows, and throw its fragments upon different parts of the plain. Break then the spine in small pieces and plant it beside the woods when you may depart, but after one moon return and visit this place again."

Obeying these directions the magician returned to his lodge, and keeping these things secret waited until the expiration of the moon. When he visited the wrestling-ground, he was astonished to find the plain filled with the long blades of new-grown corn, while on the side by the wood pumpkin-vines were growing in great luxuriance.

Delighted with this discovery he kept it secret until the summer came to a close. He again visited the wrestling-ground, where he found the corn in full ear and pumpkins of an immense size. The magician gathered some specimens of each kind to carry to the young men who were his companions at Manatoline, when a voice again addressed him:

"Masswa, you have conquered me. Had you not done so, your existence would have been forfeited. Henceforth, my body shall be nourishment for you and for all the human race."

Thus was received the Gift of Corn.

The Spectral Canoe

Ampata was the faithful companion and wife of a brave young hunter and warrior, by whom she had two children. Together with her husband and children, she lived in great happiness, always following him in all the vicissitudes of his wandering life. With him and her children she passed quiet winters in the seclusion and shelter of the forest and pleasant summers upon the banks of a river, where she and her children spent the long summer day in fishing.

After a few years her husband became a celebrated warrior; and then sorrow entered the peaceful family, for, according to the habit of his tribe, he sought another wife. This was a grievous thing to Ampata.

Her husband's reason—that it would give him influence in his tribe, as he wished to marry the chief's daughter—had no effect upon her. She fled from him to her father's lodge, taking her children.

Here the winter wore quietly away; and when the spring opened, she followed her father's band down to the Fall of Waters [Niagara Falls] where, having waited her opportunity, she embarked in a canoe with her children.

On approaching the falls, the increasing velocity of the current rendered the paddles of but little use. She rested with them suspended in her hands, while she arose and uttered this lament:

"I loved him with the love of my heart. I prepared for him with joy the fresh-killed meat and swept with boughs my lodge fire. I dressed for him the skin of the noble deer, and worked with my hand the moccasins that graced his feet. I waited, while the sun ran his daily course, for his return from the chase; and I rejoiced in my heart when I heard his footstep approach my lodge. He threw down his burden at the door. I flew to prepare food for him. He departed from me. I can live no longer. My children add to my grief. I have lifted up my voice to the Master of Life. I have asked him to take back my life. I am on the current that fulfills my prayer. I see the white foam on the water; it is my shroud. I hear the murmur from below; it is my song. Farewell!"

They saw her enter the foaming torrent. For an instant the canoe was suspended upon the brink of the Falls—then it disappeared forever.

Since then, the canoe of Ampata has sometimes been seen by moonlight plung-ing over the Falls, while strange elk and fawn are seen on the shore.

The Lynx and Hare

A lynx, almost famished from excessive hunger, met a hare one day in the woods in the winter season; but the hare was separated from its enemy by a rock upon which it stood.

The lynx began to speak to it in very smooth tones: "Wabose! Wabose!" said he, "come here, my little white one, and let us have a pleasant talk."

"Oh, no," said the hare, "I am afraid of you, and my mother told me never to talk with strangers."

"You are very pretty" replied the lynx, "and very obedient to your parents; but I am a relative of yours, and wish to send a message by you to your lodge. Come down, my pretty white one, and let me tell it to you."

The hare was pleased to be so flatteringly spoken to—and when she found the lynx to be a relative and not a stranger, she bounded down from the rock where she stood.

Alas! her "kinsman" immediately pounced upon and devoured her.

Akukojeesh, the Ground-Hog

A female ground-hog, with a numerous family, was burrowing in her *wa-uzh*, or hole in the ground, one very long winter; when her family, wearied of their protracted confinement, became impatient for the appearance of spring, and longed to see the light, and the green things of the earth.

"Mother," said they, "is it not almost spring?"

"No! no!" said she, in a cross humor, "keep still, and wait patiently; it hails and snows. Ough! it is cold; it is windy. Why should you wish to leave your warm bed?"

Now the little family, having been so answered several times by their mother, began to suspect some deception. One day, after a long absence, she came in so tired that she lay down and fell asleep.

During her sleep her mouth dropped open, into which the baby hogs slyly peeped, and they saw on her teeth the remains of the nice white bulbous roots of *mo-na-ring*, or adder's-tongue violet.

The little ones at once knew it was spring, and without disturbing their mother, who had desired to keep them in safety, cautiously left their *wa-uzh* and scampered off into the woods—and from that time saw their mother no more.

The Raccoon and Crawfish

The raccoon searches the margins of streams for shell-fish, where he is generally sure of finding the *as-shog-aish-i*, or crawfish. But at one time the crawfish would no longer venture near the shore, and the raccoon was on the point of starvation.

At length he fixed on a plan to decoy his enemy. Knowing the crawfish fed on worms, he procured a quantity of decayed wood filled with them. Stuffing the rotten wood in his mouth and ears and powdering it over his body, he lay down by the water's edge to induce the belief that he was dead.

Soon an old crawfish came out warily from the water, crawled around and over the body of his apparently deceased enemy, and rejoiced to find an end put to its murderous career. He cried out to his fellows: "Come up, my brothers and sisters, Aissibun [the raccoon] is dead; come up and eat him."

At once a great multitude gathered around. Then, to their consternation, the raccoon suddenly sprang up and devoured them every one.

While he was engaged with the broken limbs, a little female crawfish, carrying her infant sister on her back, came up seeking her relations. Finding they had all been devoured by the raccoon, she resolved not to survive the destruction of her kindred, but went boldly up to the enemy and said:

"Here, Aissibun, you behold me and my little sister. We are all alone. You have eaten up our parents and all our friends. Eat us too."

And she continued to say: "Eat us, too— *Aissibun amoon, Aissibun amoon.*"

The raccoon was ashamed. "No," said he, "I have banqueted on the largest and fattest. I will not dishonor myself with such little prey."

At this moment Manabozho, the great Light Being, happened to pass by. "Tyau," said he to the raccoon, "thou art a thief and an unmerciful dog. Get thee up into trees, lest I change thee into one of these same worm-fish; for you wast thyself a shell-fish originally, and I transformed thee."

Manabozho then took up the little supplicant crawfish and her infant sister and cast them into the stream.

"There," said he, "you may dwell. Hide yourselves under the stones; and hereafter you shall be playthings for little children."

The Boy and the Wolves— Or, the Broken Promise

In the depths of a solitary forest a hunter had built his lodge, for he was weary of the companionship of the people of his tribe; their habits of deceit and cruelty had turned his heart from them. With his family, his wife, and three children, he had selected a home in the solitude of the forest.

Years passed by while he peacefully enjoyed the quiet of his home, or the more attractive pleasures of the chase, in which he was joined by his eldest son. At length his peaceful enjoyments were interrupted. Sickness entered the solitary lodge, and the hunter was prostrated upon his couch never more to rise.

As death drew near, he addressed his family in these words:

"You," said he turning to his wife, "you,

who have been the companion of my life, shall join me in the Isle of the Blessed. You have not long to suffer. But oh, my children!" and he turned his eyes affectionately upon them, "you have just commenced life; and mark me, unkindness, ingratitude, and every wickedness is before you. I left my tribe and kindred to come to this unfrequented place because of the evils of which I have just warned you. I have contented myself with the company of your mother and yourselves, for I was solicitous that you might be kept from bad example; and I shall die contented if you, my children, promise to cherish each other, and not to forsake your youngest brother."

Exhausted with speaking, the dying hunter closed his eyes for a few moments, and then, rousing himself with a great effort, he took the hand of his two eldest children and said: "My daughter, never forsake your youngest brother. My son, never forsake your youngest brother."

"Never! never!" responded both; and the hunter sank back upon his pallet and soon expired.

His wife, according to predictions, followed him after the brief expiration of eight months; but in her last moments she reminded the two children of the promise made their father.

During the winter following their mother's death, the two elder children were exceedingly thoughtful in regard to their brother, who was a mere child and very delicate and sickly. But when the winter had passed away, the young man became restless, and at length determined to break his promise to his father and seek the village of his father's tribe.

He communicated this determination to his sister, who replied: "My brother, I cannot wonder at your desire, as we are not prohibited the society of our fellow-men; but we were told to cherish each other and protect our little brother. If we follow our own inclinations, we may forget him."

To this the young man made no reply, but, taking his bow and arrows, left the lodge and never returned.

Several moons passed after his departure, during which the girl tenderly watched over her little brother. But at length the solitude of her life became unendurable, and she began to contemplate escaping from the care of her brother and leaving him alone in his helplessness.

She gathered into the lodge a large amount of food, then said to her brother, "My brother, do not leave the lodge; I go to seek our brother, and shall soon return."

Then she went in search of the village of her tribe, where she hoped to find her elder brother.

When she reached the village, she was so delighted with the novelty of society and the pleasure of seeing others of her own age that she entirely forgot her little brother.

She found her elder brother nicely settled in life (he having married very happily) and, on receiving a proposal of marriage herself, abandoned all thought of returning to the solitary lodge in the forest.

As soon as the little brother had eaten all the food collected by his sister, he went into the woods and picked berries and dug up roots. These things satisfied his hunger as long as the weather was mild; but, when the winter drew on, he was obliged to wander about in very great distress for want of food.

He often passed his nights in the clefts and hollows of old trees, and he was glad to eat the scraps left by the wolves.

He became so fearless of those animals that he would sit by them while they devoured their prey. The animals themselves were so accustomed to him that they seemed pleased with his presence, and they always left some of their food for him. Thus the little boy lived on through the winter, succored from hunger by the wild beasts of the woods.

When the winter had passed away and the ice had melted from the Great Lake, he followed the wolves to its open shore. It happened one day that his elder brother was fishing in his canoe on the lake, and, hearing the cry of a child, he hastened to the shore, where he discovered his little brother, who was singing plaintively these lines:

Nesia, Nesia, shug wuh, gushuh!
Ne mien gun-iew! Ne mien gun-iew!
My brother, my brother!
I am turning into a wolf!
I am turning into a wolf!

At the termination of his song, he howled like a wolf. The elder brother, approaching him, was startled at seeing that the little fellow had indeed half turned into a wolf.

Running hastily forward, he shouted, "My brother, my little brother, come to me!"

But the boy fled from him, continuing to sing: "I am turning into a wolf!—*Ne mien-gun-iew! Ne mien gun-iew!*"

Filled with anguish and remorse, the elder brother continued to cry, "My brother, my little brother, come to me!"

But the more eagerly he called, the more rapidly his brother fled with him—all the while becoming more and more like a wolf, until, with a prolonged howl, his whole body was transformed; and he bounded swiftly away into the depths of the forest.

The elder brother, in the deepest sorrow, now returned to his village, where with his sister he lamented the dreadful fate of his brother until the end of his life.

The Mysterious Visitors

It was evening. A hunter's wife sat alone in her lodge, waiting for the return of her husband.

Hearing the sound of approaching footsteps, she hastily went to the door and beheld two females approaching in the darkness. She kindly bade them to enter her lodge and invited them to remain through the night. As they entered, the wife observed that they were strangers and that they were very shy, keeping their faces partially covered with the garments that they had carefully drawn about them to shade themselves from observation. In the fitful light of the fire, the portion of their faces that could be seen looked wan and emaciated, and their eyes seemed very much sunken.

"Merciful spirit!" cried a voice from the opposite part of the lodge, "There are two corpses, clothed with garments!"

The hunter's wife turned around, but seeing no one she concluded the sounds were but a sigh of wind. She trembled, however, and felt ready to sink to the earth.

Her husband now returned, and his presence dispelled her fears. He had been successful in hunting, and threw upon the ground a large, fat deer.

"Behold, what a fine fat animal!" cried the mysterious females; and they immediately ran and pulled off pieces of the whitest fat, which they ate greedily.

The hunter and his wife looked on with astonishment, but remained silent. They thought their guests might have been famished.

Next day, however, the same unusual conduct was repeated. The strange females tore off the fat from the hunter's game and devoured it with eagerness.

The third day the hunter thought he would anticipate their wants by tying up a portion of the fattest pieces for them, which he placed on the top of his load. They accepted it, but still appeared dissatisfied and went to the wife's portion and tore off more.

The hunter and his wife were surprised at such rude and unaccountable conduct, but they made no remarks, for they respected their visitors, and had observed that they had been attended with unusual good luck during their visit. Besides, the strangers were very modest in their behavior in all other respects, always seating themselves quietly in the back part of the lodge and never speaking through the day. At night they would occupy themselves in procuring wood for the lodge, and they were never known to stay out until daylight. They were never heard to laugh or jest.

The winter had nearly passed away

without anything uncommon happening, when one evening the hunter was delayed until a late hour. The moment he entered with his day's hunt and threw it at the feet of his wife, the two females began to tear the fat off in such an unceremonious manner that the wife's anger was excited. She endeavored to restrain herself, but she was unable to conceal her feelings entirely, and her looks betrayed her displeasure.

The guests observed her, and at once became reserved and appeared uneasy.

The good hunter perceived this, and inquired of his wife the cause. She assured him that she had spoken no harsh word to them.

In the night the hunter was disturbed by the sound of weeping, and he soon discovered that his guests were in great grief.

He arose on his couch and addressed them as follows: "Tell me," said he "what is it that gives you pain of mind and causes you to utter these sighs? Has my wife given you offense, or trespassed on the rights of hospitality?"

"We have been treated," they answered, "by you with kindness and affection. It is not for any slight we have received that we weep. Our mission is not to you alone. We come from the Land of the Departed Spirits to test mankind and to try the sincerity of the living. Often we have hear the bereaved say that if the dead could be restored, they would devote their lives to make them happy. We were moved by the sounds of bitter lamentations, which have reached the ears of the departed, to come upon earth and make a proof of the sincerity of those who mourn. Three moons were allotted to us by the Master of Life to make the trial. More than half the time had been successfully passed when the angry feelings of your wife indicated the irksomeness you felt at our presence and thus we have resolved to make our departure."

The two guests then continued to talk to the hunter and his wife, and, giving them instructions as to their future life, pronounced a blessing upon them.

"There is one thing which we wish to explain," said they; "it is our conduct in possessing ourselves of that delicacy that properly belonged to your wife, and which was the choicest part of the hunt. This was done as a test. Pardon us. We were the agents of the Master of Life. Peace to your dwelling!"

As the sound of their voices ceased, darkness fell over the place. The hunter and his wife, unable to see their guests, heard them leave the lodge, and soon their departing footsteps were lost in the distance.

The Evil Spirit: A Mistake of the Master of Life

Although a belief in the existence of a personal devil is common in the religious concepts of humankind, the traditional Medicine people did not conceive of an omnipresent evil spirit that had been created by the Master of Life for the purpose of tempting humankind or of destroying it. They perceived the origin of the dread entity as a mistake of the Creator, which is probably as wise a way of quieting the haunting question of the origin of evil as that taken by making philosophers and theologians.

Dealing with evil and negativity is a great part of the challenge of walking in balance on the Earth Mother. Evil cannot be ignored, and it cannot be hidden. Neither can one run away from its poison and its deceit. The Dark Side of the Force must be confronted with discernment, discipline, and direct action.

Metowac [Long Island] was formerly a vast level plain, that, having once been overwashed by the sea, was exceedingly smooth and seemed like a large, sandy table. It was upon this plain that the Master of Life worked out his creations undisturbed, for the sea encircled him on every side.

Here he formed those early creations which were of such gigantic size that he himself found it difficult to control them; for he always gave to each certain elements, the laws of which they controlled until he took back their life to himself. Here also he would frequently try his creations, and, giving them life, would set them in motion upon the island. Then, if they did not suit him, he would withdraw their life from them before they escaped.

It was in this manner that the Master of Life constructed his animals:

He placed four cakes of clay at proper distances upon the ground, then slowly worked upwards as one constructs a canoe. After the animal was finished, he dried it a long time in the sun; then, opening a place in its side, he entered it and remained many days. When he came forth the shivering creature swayed from side to side, shaking the island by its motion. If his appearance was pleasing in his master's sight, he was allowed to depart upon the north side of the island, passing through the sea to the opposite shore.

At one time the Master of Life occupied himself a long time in building a creature of marvelous size, which was an object of great curiosity to the little spirit entities, who often visited it. The Forest Spirits found great amusement in hiding behind its ears or capering along its back—sometimes sitting within its mouth, perched upon its lower teeth—while the foolish little things thought the Master of Life could not see him, for he was deeply absorbed in his work. But the Master of Life can see all things; he can see through all the creatures he has made.

Notwithstanding the pains with which the Master of Life worked over the animal, it proved too large for his taste. Besides, he was unwilling to give life to a creature that would have so much strength—and so he concluded to leave it where it was. Thus neglected, the weight of the monster caused it partly to sink down into the island, where it hung supported by its head and tail.

After this the Master of Life amused himself by making very small creatures. On finding that they were not so attractive as the wee spirit people of the forest, however, he would receive their life into himself, then cast their bodies within the frame of the gigantic unfinished animal. In this way a great variety of oddly shaped things were hid together in what was called the Roncommon [Place of Fragments].

One day the Master of Life molded two pieces of clay into two large feet, like those of a panther. He slipped his own feet within them, and was pleased to find their tread was light and springy, so that he might walk with noiseless speed. Taking his feet out, he made a pair of very long legs. These he caused to walk, and finding their motion was easy, he fastened upon them a round body, covered with large scales, like an alligator's.

But the figure doubled forward; so, catching up a black snake that was gliding by, the Master of Life fastened it to the body and let it wind itself about a sapling nearby —which not only held the body upright, but made a very good tail. The Master of Life had made the shoulders broad and strong, like those of a buffalo, covering them with hair, and making the neck very short and thick and full at the back.

Thus far the Master of Life had worked with little thought, but when he came to the head he reflected a long time. He took a round ball of clay into his lap and worked it over with much care. Musing deeply, patting the while the top of the ball, he almost forgot the work to be done—for he was considering the panther-feet and buffalo-neck. Thus the ball became very broad and low.

Reflecting upon the sports of the Forest Spirits, who had made the eye-sockets of the great unfinished animal a sort of gateway out of which they leaped with much merriment, he concluded to make the eyes like those of a lobster, so the creature could see on all sides. The forehead he made broad and low. The jaws were set with ivory teeth, heavy and strong, with gills on either side. The nose was like the beak of a vulture, and a tuft of porcupine quills made the scalp-lock.

Here the Master of Life paused. Holding

the head out at arm's length, he turned it from side to side. He passed it rapidly through the air and saw the gills rise and fall, the eyes whirl, and the beak look keen.

He became very sad. He had never made such a creature, one with two feet—a creature who should stand upright and see upon all sides—yet he resolutely placed the head upon a pair of shoulders.

Night now approached, and with it a tempest arose. Heavy clouds obscured the moon, and the wind swept over the island in fierce gusts. The beasts of the forest began to roar, and the bats skimmed through the air. A panther approached the great beast and with one foot raised and bent inward looked at the image, smelling of the feet that were like his own. A vulture swooped down and made a dash at the monster's beak. Then came a porcupine, a lizard, and a serpent—each attracted by a likeness to itself in the hug creature.

The Master of Life veiled his face many hours, while the strong wind swept by him. Seeing that like attracts like, the idea grew into his mind that he would have some creatures who should be made, not like the things of the earth, but after his own image. Many days and nights he reflected upon this.

He saw all things. Now, as he raised his head, he noticed that a bat lit upon the forehead of the image, its great wings spreading on each side. The Master of Life rose up, took the bat, and held its wings over the image's head.

Since that day, the bat, when he rests, hangs his head downwards.

The Master of Life then twisted the body of the bat from its wings, taking its life. As he held the bat over the image's head, the whole thin part of the bat fell down over the creature's forehead, like a hooded serpent. The Master of Life did not cut off the face below, but went on, making a chin and lips that were firm and round, that they might shut in a forked tongue and ivory teeth. He knew that, with the lips and chin, it would smile when life was given it.

The image was now entirely completed, except the arms; and the Master of Life saw that, with a chin, it must have arms and hands. He grew more grave, for he had never given hands to any creature; but he did not hesitate. He made the hands and arms very beautiful, after the fashion of his own.

The work was then finished, but the Master of Life took no pleasure in it.

He began to wish he had not given it hands. Might it not, when trusted with life, create? Might it not thwart even himself?

He looked at the image. The Master of Life saw what it would do, should he give it life. He knew all things.

He now put fire into the image, and a red glow passed through and through it. But fire is not life.

Terrible and fierce was its aspect. The lobster-eyes were like burning coals, and the scales of its body glistened with fierce light.

The Master of Life opened the side of the image. He did not enter.

By his command the image walked around the island of Metowac, that he might see it move.

He now put a little life into it; but he did not take out the fire. He saw that the creature's aspect was very terrible, but that it could smile in such a manner that it ceased to be ugly.

The Master of Life dwelt long upon these things, and finally decided that such a creature—made up mostly of beasts, with hands of power, a chin lifting its head upwards, and lips holding all things within themselves—must not live.

Upon this decision he took the image in his hands and cast it into Roncommon, the Place of Fragments; *but he forgot to take out the life.*

The fall was great, and the creature lay a long time without motion among the discarded creations that had been thrown there lifeless.

When a long time had elapsed, the Master of Life heard a great noise in Roncommon; and, looking in, he saw the ugly image sitting up, trying to put together the old fragments that had been cast within the cavern.

He gathered a large heap of sand and stones and closed up the mouth of Roncommon.

The noise now grew louder. When a few days had passed, the earth began to shake, and hot smoke issued from the ground. The spirits of sea and land crowded to Metowac to see what was the cause of the disturbance.

For the first time, it occurred to the Master of Life that he had forgotten to take the life from the image he had cast within the cavern; and he therefore came to watch the result of his mistake.

While he and the spirit beings stood close by the cavern listening to the noise, which continually increased, suddenly there was a great rising of the sand and stones; the sky grew dark with wind and dust, fire ran along the ground, and water gushed high into the air.

Terrified by these sights the spirit beings retired with fear. With a great rushing sound, the image came forth from the cavern. His life had grown strong within him, fed by the burning fire. At the sight of him every earthly creature trembling hid, while, filling the air with their cries, the spirit beings fled from the island, shrieking: "*Matchí Manitto! Matchí Manitto!*"

It was the Evil Spirit.

The First Battle Between Inigoria and Inigohatea, Good and Evil

The Great Mystery created Good and Evil, brothers. The one went forth to make beautiful things, and all pleasant places were the products of his labor. The other busied himself in thwarting his brother's plans. He made hard and flinty places in the earth and caused bad fruits to grow. In truth, he was continually employed in making mischief throughout the whole universe.

Good had patiently endeavored to re-pair the effects of Evil's mischievous works; but, finding his labor would never be completed, one day, while thinking over this, he determined to destroy his brother. Not wishing to use violence, he meditated some time as to the means that he would use to cause his death. At length he concluded upon a plan, and giving to his brother, proposed a race with him. To this, Evil consented, and together they decided upon a place for the race.

"First tell me," said Good, "that which you dislike the most."

"Bucks' horns," replied Evil, "and now tell me what is most hurtful to you!"

"Indian grass-braid," answered Good.

Evil then procured grass-braid in large quantities from his grandmother, Mishiken, who had created it. This he placed in Good's racecourse, thickly strewing it upon the ground, and hanging it all along the trees—while Good filled his brother's course with bucks' horns.

The question now arose between the brothers, who should start first in the race. After some dispute, Good was allowed the preference. He accordingly started, Evil following.

After running some distance, feeling fatigued, Good stooped, gathered some of the grass-braid, and ate of it. Such a meal invigorated him so much that he tired out Evil, who, panting and breathless, cried out to his brother, requesting him to stop and wait for him. Good was unwilling to do this, and so, continued his way until he reached the goal.

In the meantime Evil toiled along, encountered everywhere by the dreaded horns, until at last he besought his brother to relieve him from going any farther.

But no, Good insisted on his running his course, and at sunset, Evil, wearied out, fell down in his path and was quickly dispatched by his brother with one of the horns.

The victor then returned to the lodge of their grandmother, whom Good found in an ill-humor—for she loved Evil best and was greatly grieved by his defeat.

Now at night Evil came and requested

permission to enter the lodge, but his brother denied him admission.

"Then," said Evil, "I go to the northwest, and you shall see no more; but all who follow will be in the same state in which I am. They will never return to earth. Death shall keep them forever."

Thereupon he departed to the Land of Silence.

The Works of the Evil Spirit

While the Great Mystery had been at work, the Evil Spirit was asleep. He now awoke; and on finding how much the Great Mystery had created, he went to work himself—quite sure of being able to do as much.

His first effort was to try to make an Indian; but, through some mistake in the ingredients, an ape was produced.

He then endeavored to make a black bear, and it turned out a miserable grizzly creature.

He then made several serpents, but they were filled with poison.

He commenced work in the vegetable line and created a set of useless herbs. He made a few ugly and distorted trees and sowed myriads of thistles.

To complete the sum of his machinations, he tempted the creations of the Great Mystery to evil, and he made some of the Indians steal and murder and lie.

One day the Evil Spirit and the Great Mystery will have a battle. At that time, there will be darkness four days and nights, there will be thunders and lightnings, and then the wicked will go to the Evil Spirit. At that time the Earth will be destroyed again by a great flood of waters; but the Great Mystery, who will always exist, will restore it again.

Origin of War

One hundred and eighteen summers had elapsed since the creation of the Earth and its inhabitants, when the Great Mystery looked down upon the planet for the first time since the beginning. He then saw old men and women coming out of their lodges, gray-headed and stooping; and when they issued forth they fell into pieces from extreme age.

The Great Mystery then thought that he had made the Indians to live too long, and that they increased too rapidly.

He changed his first plan and sent four Spirits of Thunder to tell the the Indians that they must fight. They obeyed; after which they decreased rapidly.

Upon the death of those Indians who were killed in battle, the Great Mystery placed their souls near himself.

Boshkwadosh

A man who was alone in the world had wandered about from place to place until he was so weary that he lay down and fell asleep.

In his sleep he heard a voice saying: "Nosis! Nosis! My grandchild! My grandchild!"

Upon awakening, he actually heard it repeated. Looking around, he discovered a tiny animal, hardly big enough to be seen with the naked eye.

While speculating whether a voice could come from so diminutive a source, the animal cried again: "My grandson, I am Boshkwadosh. Tell me, why are you so desolate? Listen to me, and you shall find friends and be happy. You must take me up and bind me to your body and never put me aside, and success will attend you through life."

The man took the little animal and placed him carefully in a little sack, which he bound around his waist. Then he set out in search of someone who would be a suitable companion for him.

He walked a long distance without seeing man or animal. At length he came where there had been a tree felled; and going over a hill, he saw a large town in the center of a plain. The town was divided by a wide road, and he noticed that the lodges on one side of the road were uninhabited, while on the other side they were filled with people.

He walked without hesitation into the town, and the people all rushed out from their lodges, crying: "Why, here is Anishinaba, the being we have heard so much about! See his eyes and his teeth in a half-circle, the Wyaukenarbedaid! How queer he is formed!"

Amidst their shouting, the king's son appeared, the Mudjèkewis, and, greeting him with great kindness, conducted him to his father's lodge, where he was received by the king with much attention. He was even presented one of the king's beautiful daughters.

Anishinaba—for this was this man's name—soon discovered that this tribe passed much of their time in play and sports and trials of strength. After he was refreshed and rested, they invited him to join with them in these amusements.

The first trial they desired him to make was that of frost. At some distance from the village there was a large body of frozen water, and the trial consisted in lying down naked on the ice and seeing who could endure the longest.

Anishinaba, accompanied by two young men, went out and lay his face upon the ice, according to their directions, the young men doing the same. At first there was much laughter between the youths, and they would call out to him, with many jests and jeers, to which he made no answer. He felt a manifest warmth from the belt, and he was quite sure of his success.

About midnight, the two young men were quiet, and he called to them: "What!" said he, "are you benumbed already? I am just beginning to feel the cold."

All was still. Waiting until daybreak, he went to them and found them both quite dead. But to his great surprise, they were transformed into buffalo cows.

He tied them together, however, and carried them in triumph to the village. His victory was hailed with pleasure by Mudjèkewis only, for all the others had wished his death. This did not disturb Anishinaba, especially since, through his victory, two persons were mysteriously added to the silent lodges on the uninhabited side of the village.

Anishinaba now was invited to another trial, which was of speed, in which he was equally successful, being borne as upon wings to the goal, outspeeding all others with the swiftness of the *ka-ka-ke* (the sparrow-hawk).

The villagers, however, were not yet convinced of his superior prowess, and they desired him once more to go through the trial of frost.

Previous to the trial he lay down to rest, untying his belt, which he placed beneath his hand. Anishinaba slept some time. On awakening, he sprang up hastily and, feeling full of vigor and courage, hastened to the ice without recalling that he had taken off the belt. Then, alas, the cold entered his body, and by morning he was frozen to death.

Mudjèkewis bemoaned the fate of his friend, and the wife of Anishinaba was inconsolable. As she lay in her lodge in deep sorrow, she heard a groan, which was many times repeated through the night.

In the morning she went to the place from whence she thought the sound might have issued, and there, within the grass, she found the belt with the mystic sack.

"*Aubishin*, untie me!" cried a voice from the sack. As she carefully examined it for the seam, the voice continued to vociferate, "Aubishin! Aubishin!"

At last, having succeeded in opening the sack, she was surprised to see a large naked animal, smaller than a new-born mouse, without a vestige of hair, except at the tip of its tail. The little beast was so weak that it could crawl only a little way and then rest. At each rest, however, it would shake itself, and, at every shake it grew in dimensions, until, finally, it became as large as a dog.

When it had attained this size, it ran

quickly to the village, and in great haste collected the bones of Anishinaba, which were strewn about in the different lodges. As fast as the bones were collected, he adjusted them together in their natural position until, at length, he had formed a complete skeleton.

The strange creature then placed himself before the skeleton and uttered a hollow, low, continuous howl at which the bones united themselves compactly together. The mysterious beast then modulated his howl, and the bones knit together. The third howl brought sinews upon the bones; the fourth and softest howl brought flesh.

The beast then turned his head upwards, looking into the sky, and gave a howl that caused the people of the village to tremble, and the earth itself shook; then breath entered the body.

Taking a few respirations Anishinaba arose, saying: "*Hy, ko!* I have overslept myself. I shall be too late for the trial."

"Trial!" said the mysterious animal. "You neglected my advice and were defeated. You were frozen to death, and your body broken into fragments; for, when you undertook the trial of frost, you ungratefully forgot me; but by my skill I have returned you to life, and now I will declare myself to you."

Thereupon the strange animal shook himself many times. At every shake, he grew larger and larger, until he seemed to touch the sky.

"I should fill the Earth, were I to exert my utmost power, and all therein would not satisfy the desires of my appetite. It is useless, therefore, for me to exhibit my strength, and henceforth I give unto you power over all animals. They shall be your food, as they all belong to me."

So saying, the marvellous creature vanished from sight.

Seek Your Own Vision

Here is a guided meditation that we have used at our seminars and Medicine Wheel gatherings throughout the United States and Canada. It is one that we have found very effective for leading groups into a simulated vision quest experience. It is one that you can use in by prerecording your voice and by becoming your own guide through the experience. Or you may read it aloud to a trusted friend or loved one, and then have that same individual read it for you and lead you through the experience.

Enter a state of very relaxed frame of mind. When you have reached a deep level, when you have gone deep, deep, within—moving toward the very center of essence—begin to tell yourself that you have the ability to visualize in your mind the conditions of your vision quest.

Tell yourself that you have the ability to tap into the eternal transmission of universal truth from which you may draw power and strength. You have the ability to evolve as a spiritual being.

Visualize yourself as a native American man or woman on a vision quest. Focus your thoughts on your performance of some mundane, monotonous physical task.

Perhaps like so many young native American men and women on a vision quest, you have found a small clearing in the forest which has a number of rocks of various sizes at one end of the nearly barren area. Pick up one of the rocks and carry it to the opposite side of the clearing.

In your mind, see yourself carrying the rock. See yourself placing the rock down on the ground and turning around to get another rock.

See yourself picking up a new rock, carrying it slowly to the other side of the clearing, and then another rock, and another, back and forth. Back and forth, over and over again.

Know and understand that you are performing this task for the sole purpose of depleting the physical self with monotonous exercise.

Know and understand that you are distracting the unconscious mind with dull activity, that you are doing this to free the Essential Self within you, so that it can soar free of the physical body.

Feel now your body becoming very, very tired.

Your body is feeling very heavy. It feels very, very dull.

You have no aching muscles or sore tendons, but you are very, very tired. Your physical body is exhausted.

See yourself lying down on the blanket to rest, to relax.

Slowly you become aware of a presence. Someone has approached you and has come to stand next to you.

As you look up at the figure, you see that it is a most impressive individual. It is a man who is looking at you with warmth and compassion.

And now you notice that he has been joined by a woman who is equally impressive, almost majestic in appearance.

She smiles at you, and you feel somehow as if she stands before you enveloped in the Great Mother vibration.

Before you can open your mouth to speak, the man and woman fade from your side. They simply disappear.

You realize that they were spirits, that they came to you from the spirit world to demonstrate to you that, in many ways, on many levels, you have a subtle, yet intense, partnership with the world of spirits. The spirit man and spirit woman have given you a visual sign of the reality of this oneness with all spiritual forms of life.

You have but a moment to ponder the significance of the spirit visitation when you become aware of two globes of bluish white light moving toward you. You are not afraid, for you sense a great spiritual presence approaching you.

As you watch in great expectation, the first glow of bluish white light begins to assume human form.

As the light swirls and becomes solid, you behold before you a man or a woman whom you regard as a whole person, a saint, a master, an illumined one. This figure, so beloved to you, gestures to your left side.

As you turn, you are astonished to see a marvelous link-up with other holy figures from all times, from all places, from all cultures. You see that these personages form a beautiful spiritual chain from prehistory to the present—and without doubt, the future.

The holy one smiles benevolently, then bends over you and touches your shoulder gently. The holy one's forefinger lightly touches your eyes, your ears, then your mouth.

You know within that this touching symbolizes that you are about to see and to hear a wondrous revelation, which you must share with others.

As the holy figure begins to fade from your perception, the second globe of bluish white light begins to materialize in human form.

The entity that forms before you now may be very familiar to you. You may very likely have seen this entity in your dreams, for this is your guide. One who has always loved you just as you are. This is one with unconditional love who is concerned completely with your spiritual evolution.

You feel totally relaxed, at peace, at one with your guide. You feel totally loved.

Your guide is now showing you something important. Your guide's heads are holding something for you to see.

It is an object which you can clearly identify, an object which will serve as a symbol that you are about to receive a meaningful and important teaching in your dreams.

Whenever you see this symbol in your dreams, you will understand that an important and significant teaching will instantly follow.

The symbol fades from your sight, but you will remember it.

Now, in a great rush of color and light, you are finding yourself elevated in spirit. You know that your guide has taken you to a higher vibrational level. You have moved to a dimension where nonlinear, cyclical time flows around you.

From your previous limited perspective of Earth time, linear time, you are aware that you now exist in a timeless realm in Eternal Now.

Stretching before you is something that appears to be a gigantic tapestry, a tapestry that has been woven of multi-colored living lights, lights that are pulsating, throbbing with life.

The energy of the Great Mystery touches your inner knowing, and you are made aware that you are becoming one with the great pattern of all life.

In a marvelous, pulsating movement of beautiful lights and living energy, your soul feels a unity with all living things.

You see before you now an *animal*, any animal.

You become one with its essence.

You become one with this level of awareness.

Be that animal.

Be that level of energy expression.

See before you a *bird,* any bird.

Now become one with its essence. Become one with its level of awareness.

Be that bird.

Be that level of energy expression.

See before you a *creature of the waters,* any creature.

Become one with its essence.

Become one with its level of awareness.

Be that marine creature.

Be that level of energy expression.

See before you an *insect*—any insect crawling or flying.

Become one with its essence.

Become one with its level of awareness.

Be that insect.

Be that level of energy expression.

See before you a *plant*—any flower, tree, grass, or shrub.

Become one with its essence.

Become one with its level of awareness.

Be that plant.

Be that level of energy expression.

Know now that you are one with the unity of all plant and animal essence.

Know now that you forever bear responsibility to all plant and animal life.

You are one with all things that walk on two legs or four, with all things that fly, with all things that crawl, with all things that grow in the soil, or sustain themselves in the waters.

Listen carefully as your guide begins to tell you your secret name, your spirit name, the name that only you will know, that only you and your guide will share. It is the name by which your guide will contact you.

Hear that name now.

And now your guide is showing you the image of an animal, a plant, a bird, a water creature, an image of one of the little brother or sisters other than humankind.

Focus upon that creature.

See it's beauty. Become one with its beauty.

Know that this animal, this creature, is now your totem—that symbol which will come to you often in dreams and represent the spirit of yourself on another level of reality.

See before you another person, a man, a woman, young or old.

Go into that person.

Become one with that person's essence.

Become one with that person's level of awareness.

Be that person.

Be that level of energy expression.

Know now that it is never your place to judge another expression of humankind. Know now that you have a common brotherhood and sisterhood with all of humankind. Remember always that you must do unto your brothers and sisters as you would have them do to you. Remember always that the great error is to in any way prevent another's spiritual evolution.

At this eternal second in the energy of the Eternal Now, at this vibrational level of oneness with all living things, at this frequency of awareness of unity with the cosmos, your guide is permitting you to receive a great teaching vision of something about which you need to know for your good and your gaining.

Receive this great vision now.

You will awaken at the count of five, filled with memories of your great vision quest.

When you awaken, you will feel morally elevated; you will feel intellectually illuminated. You will know that your spiritual essence is immortal. You will no longer fear death. You will no longer experience guilt or a sense of sin. You will feel filled with great charm and personal magnetism. You will feel better and healthier than ever before in your life, and you will feel a great sense of unity with all living things.

One, two, three, four, five, awake!

American Indian Power Symbols

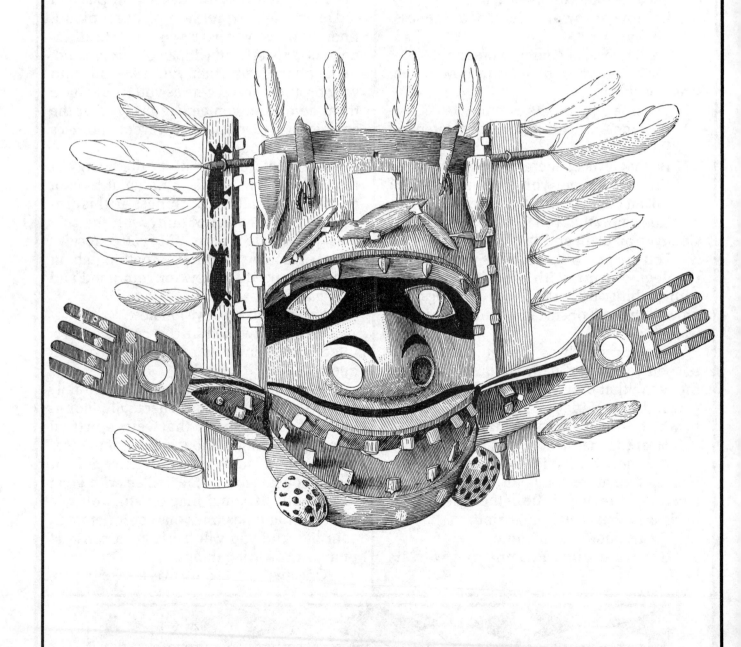

Breath Master

This power symbol represents the Breath Master, The Creator, the Great Mystery. It is His Breath and the fire of his heart that transmits the miracle of growing, expanding energy to the process of ever-renewing nature.

The symbol of this creative life force is an oval figure with small semicircles at its ends and sides. As these semicircles are also used on either side of an oval in the common symbol of the Sun, thus designating its ears, it may be that the organs of hearing that have been placed on all sides of the Breath Master represent His omnipotent ability to hear from all sides.

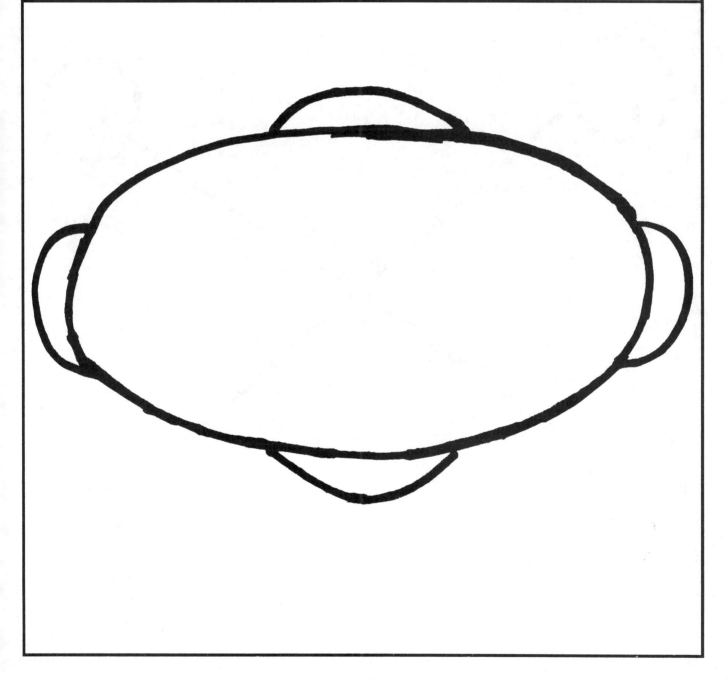

The Four Spirits of the Winds

The Winnebago describe the sentinels of the four points of the compass in this manner:

Manabozho, the great culture bearer and Being of Light, stands in the East and presides over the winds from that quarter. Animiki, the spirit of thunder, stands in the West. Menengawa, represented as a butterfly, rules in the South. Moho koko, the owl spirit, manages the North.

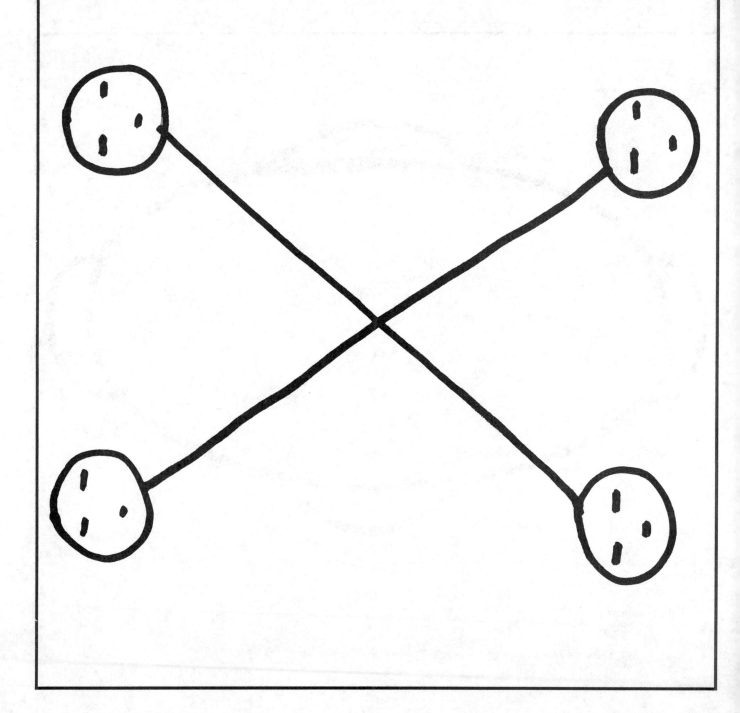

The Thunderbird

The great Thunderbird is the most common representation of Animiki, the spirit being of thunder. His wings are the dark pinions that can hide the face of the Sun.

Medicine priests often report the sighting of the Thunderbird, whose wings rattle the very skies with the roar of thunder.

Thunder is representative of supernatural power to nearly all people. The Romans held it to be the weapon of Jupiter. In the Scandinavian cosmology, the god Thor is called "The Thunderer."

The sound of thunder is mentioned in the Old Testament as accompanying the voice of God, and it is expressive of omnipotence. In Milton's *Paradise Lost,* Jesus the Son of God uses thunder as a weapon to quell the rebellious Satan.

Thunder People are prophetic, responsible individuals, who forthrightly speak the truth.

The Thunder Spirit

In this power symbol of the Thunder Spirit, the head is a parallelogram, representing fire, from which radiate four rays. The spirit being holds the mystic circle in one hand and an arrow in the other.

The Star Beings

Most of the tribes believed the stars to be the dwelling places of spiritual beings who had a connection with, and a mystical relationship to, human souls. In essence, one sought an intimate interaction with a guiding spirit from his or her own personal star.

Various understandings were found among the different Indian nations regarding the Pleiades. Some tribes believed them to be animated spirits of both sexes and referred to them as "the Dancers."

Many of the nations claimed that their ancestors—or their place of origin—came from the stars.

In this power symbol, the circles and the curved lines are the spirits of the stars and the sky.

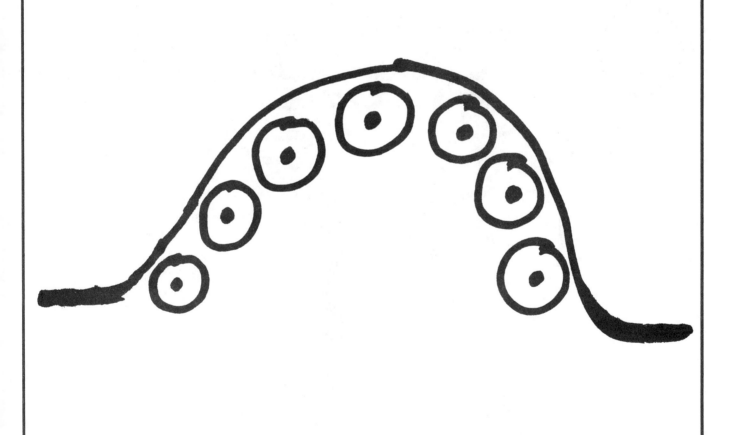

Wahundedan—She Who Overcomes Adversity

Although this powerful Dakota spirit being originally represented an entity dedicated to war, Wahundedan may also be cast as one who overcomes the most severe tests and emerges triumphant. It would seem that this is a much more positive application of this great energy.

Wahundedan's guidance was sought by the warriors as they prepared for battle. It was she who would instruct them how to conduct themselves, how to achieve success in their venture. She is most often represented with hoops on her arms and seven balls in the cap upon her head. She carries a hatchet, a war axe, which deflects the arrows of the enemy.

Her triangular cap represents a balance of mind, body, and spirit. The seven balls are in imitation of the seven tufts worn by the warrior upon his return from a successful encounter. The four circles represent the spirals of time and life and the number most sacred to the American Indians.

Fire—Mystical Link Between the Natural and the Supernatural Worlds

Life-sustaining fire was viewed as a mystery by the Indian people. Medicine priests regarded it as a mystical link between the natural and the supernatural worlds, and they believed that spirits were able to dwell within the leaping flames.

Often, in starting a fire, the wing of a white bird would be used to fan the glowing sparks.

The Cherokee believed that fire was an intermediate spirit between humans and the Sun.

In many tribes, a child was waved over fire immediately after its birth. Hunters moved their mocassins over flames to grant them protection from the bites of poisonous snakes.

Fire was regarded as an active, intelligent being, and certain tribes spoke of fire having been born or brought into creation along with them.

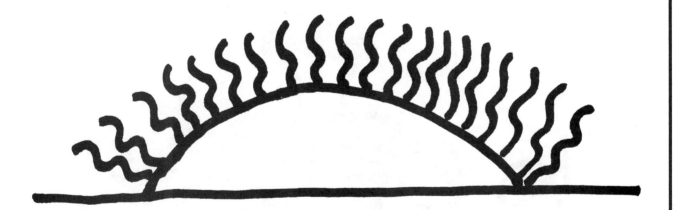

Unkatahe—The Transformer

Many of the eastern tribes had a legend that involved a most remarkable entity that resided in the depths of the great waters and presided over the fluctuations of the human soul. The creature was called Unkatahe, and it was believed that the being had power over the transformation of the soul together with the diseases that afflicted the physical body.

Unkatahe wears crescents on his feet. On his head, which is comprised of the emblematic circle, he bears horns which denote the Moon and from which rises the spiral fire. The black front-line represents Death. In the depiction of Unkatahe we may perceive the Indian's idea of the influence of the Moon over Death, and the relationship of water to Life, as this mystic creature is always portrayed as a denizen of water.

The Lodge of the Star Spirits

This power symbol represents the Medicine dwelling of the star spirits. Medicine Priests called upon such entities for assistance in determining the illness of their patient and in proclaiming the proper path for their people to follow.

The lodge is drawn in the form of the sacred triangle upon which is set the cross of the Four Winds. The circles within indicate that the Medicine Lodge is filled with star spirits who have descended to help their beloved ones on the Earth Mother.

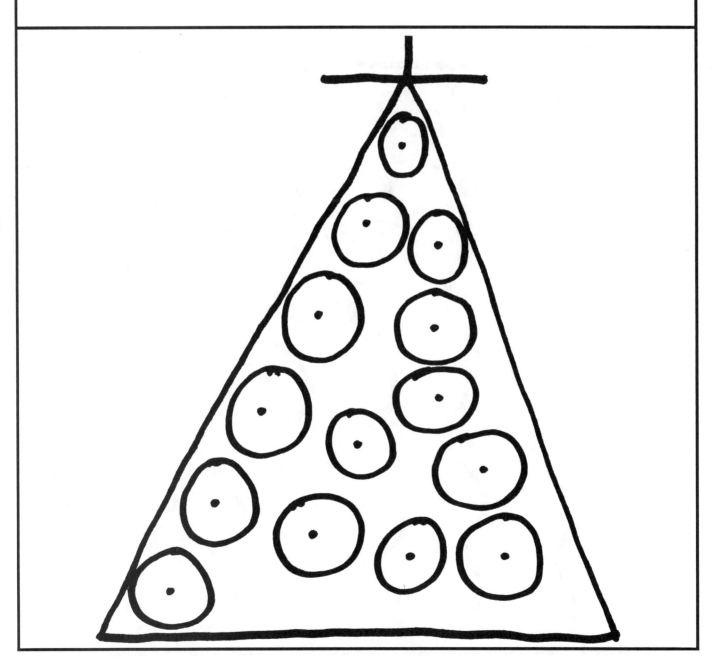

The Sacred Star Rays of Spiritual Transformation

Nearly all tribes believed that each person possessed his or her own guiding Star Spirit. Because personal will was attributed to each star, it was also believed that the star-rays could help bring about spiritual transformation. This conscious force was directed by a superior power, perhaps the Breath Master or the Great Mystery.

The power symbol is composed of a straight line which indicates the sidereal heavens. Beneath it are two lines of dots which represent the stars in their multitude. The short, wavy, perpendicular lines symbolize the celestial influence of the Star Beings upon human life.

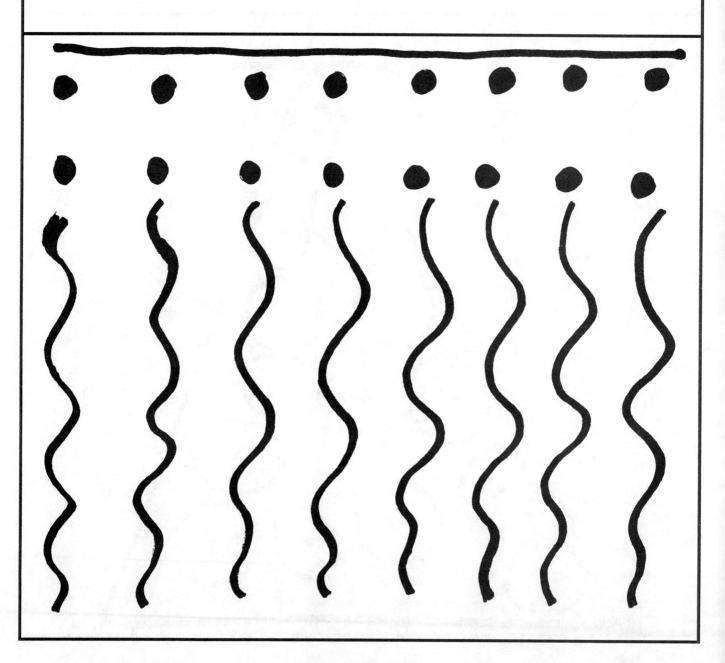

The Symbol of the Prophet

Among all living beings there are few creatures that inspire more worshipful thoughts than the winged ones of the air. It has often been observed that the flight of a bird arouses a mysterious instinct of soul. As a bird soars through limitless space, it frequently occurs to the observer that the winged one may be a messenger for holy ones, a messenger that might impart sacred knowledge to those who prepare properly, reverently, and cautiously to receive such privileged information.

And thus, the power symbol of the prophet, a drawing that blends human and bird, and transforms the arms of the seer into two birds that relay prophecy to each ear. Caution must therefore be advised, so that the prophet may correctly interpret any possible cross-communication. Many tribes, such as the Chippewa, have traditions that tell of birds that serve as agents of creation; and the winged ones became prophets of religious ceremony among most of the native people.

The journal of an early Roman Catholic priest records that the first time that the Amerindian members of his California mission saw the representation of a dove over the altar, they asked if it was the Christians' Thunderbird.

Manabozho: Great Light Being—Culture Bearer for the Indians

Some scholars of the American Indian have referred to Manabozho as their "God of Light," who appears in human form.

Legend tells of a great Spirit Being from the stars who visited Earth and who became enamored of an Indian maiden. Their first born son was Manabozho, the friend of the human race. The second born son was Chibiabos, who has the care of the dead and who presides over the Country of Souls. The third son was Wabassa, who went immediately to the North and became a powerful entity there. The fourth son was Shokanipok, the Man of Flint, who turned a hard heart toward the human people and who challenged his oldest brother, Manabozho, for supremacy on Earth.

After a long struggle, Manabozho defeated his cruel brother and traveled the Earth distributing all manner of arts and advancements to humankind. He gave them lances, bows, and arrow points. He showed them how to fashion fish nets. He taught them how to plant gourds and corn. He demonstrated the gifts of singing and dancing. He also killed the last of the ancient monsters, whose bones are now found deep in the earth; and he removed many snares that had been set for humans by the Evil Spirit.

Manabozho is spoken of as the Defender in Indian history. He rescued the people from their enemies, the enormous serpents and monstrous animals that infested the primeval world. It was the benevolent Messiah-like Manabozho who *recreated* the Earth and who instituted Great Medicine practices for humankind.

The power symbol of Manabozho is depicted with horns attached to a circular helmet that suggests an unbroken circle of Oneness with all humankind. He holds a serpent fast in his fist, thus representing his power over the monsters of old, as well as the treacherous creatures of today. The crescent-shaped horns, the black triangle on his chest, and the serpent also suggest an association with the Moon deity and point toward Manabozho's other-worldly origins. As the Moon brings light to the darkness of the night, so did the coming of Manabozho help to bring illumination to the primitive darkness of Earth.

Yohewah—She Who Raises the Grasses and the Green, Growing Things

This power symbol represents the Spirit Being of grasses and vegetable growth. The figure bears upon her head the sacred parallelogram, the emblem of fire, from which rise four rays of warmth, necessary for the life force to enter seeds. The bow and the arrow, upon which is fixed a small round object, suggests the Thunder Being who gives rain in order to promote growth in the vegetable world. The three lines radiating downward indicate the flow of life energy into the Earth Mother. In the hand of that same arm, Yohewah holds a sprig of spring grass.

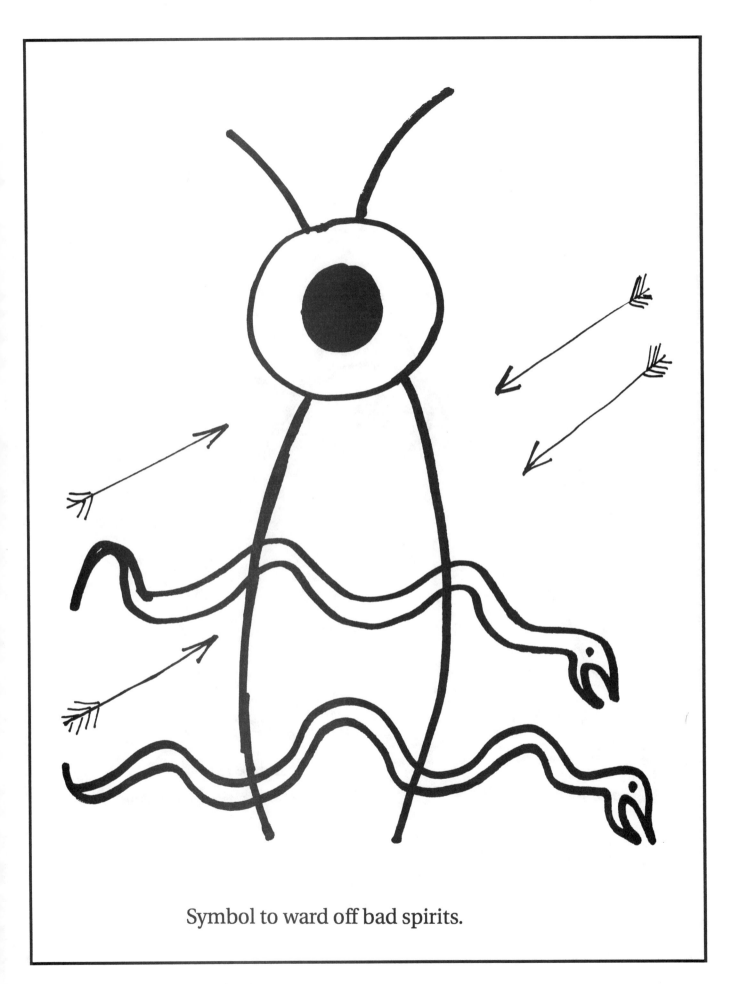

Symbol to ward off bad spirits.

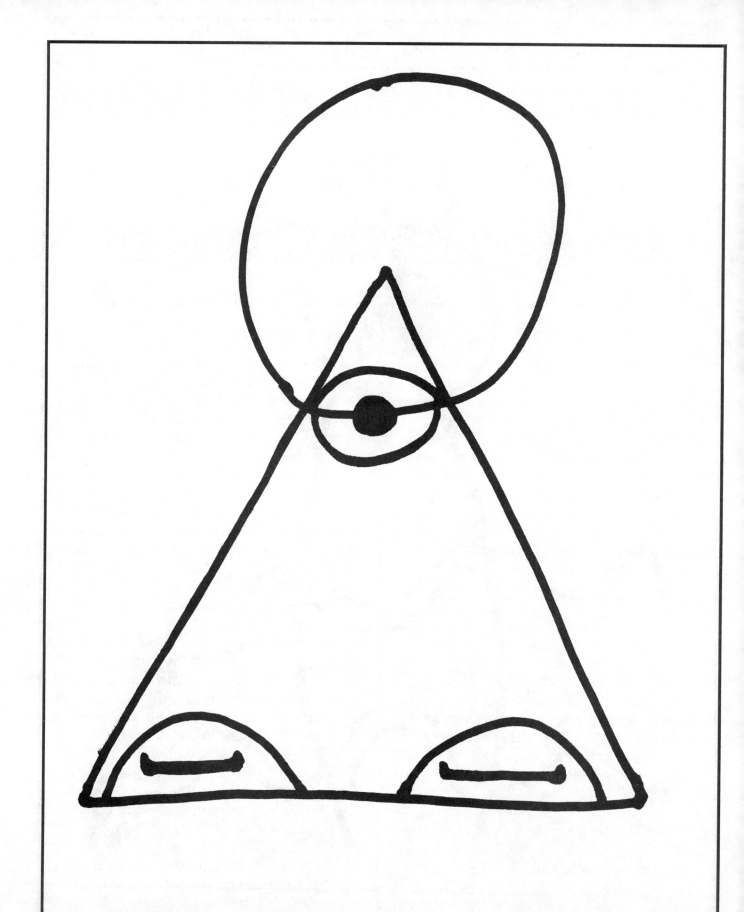

Symbol of first spirit being who came before humans.

American Indian Medicine & the Coming Earth Changes

The "medicine" of which we speak in this book has nothing to do with prescribed pills and tonics from your local pharmacy—and it deals only indirectly with herbs and dietal regimens. The Medicine to which this book refers deals specifically with the spiritual path of the traditional American Indian. We feel the information relayed by the Medicine people from the various tribes is of vital concern to contemporary humankind. Even the ancient myths and legends, which we recounted in this book, have an enormous value as stories with truths and powers to be applied in modern living.

Sometimes we are rebuffed by people who, upon hearing us speak of Medicine Power, accuse us of advocating a return to superstition and primitive life styles. This, of course, is not the case at all.

In our opinion, the cause of so many adult, civilized, and sophisticated men's and women's neuroses is their conscious or unconscious recognition that they have lost their mystical communion with Nature—the Earth Mother—and their sense of Oneness with the God-Force—the Great Mystery—that pervades all things. We believe that a practice of Medicine Power—and it can be blended harmoniously with whatever spiritual path you presently follow—can permit one to regain—at least symbolically—that state of union for which we feel so much longing and nostalgia.

While it would be quite foolish and wrong to apply primitive modes of action in our contemporary scientific paradigm of Space Age technology or to engage in superstitious practices in an attempt to establish a separate reality, Medicine Power presents us with an excellent means of dealing directly with the unconscious and of making firm contact with the archetypal psyche.

We believe that modern man desperately needs to re-establish meaningful union with the primitive layer of the psyche that views and understands life as an organic whole. To be primitive in our relationships with the external world of consensual reality which we all share is to be superstitious. But to be primitive in relation to the inner-world of the psyche is to be wise.

Our continued existence and survival on this planet depend on the extent to which the world is guided by spiritual men and women. We must never cease to reflect upon existence, God, and goodness. We must never permit the arts to die. We must not forsake the heritage of spirituality that has been bequeathed to us over thousands of years. We must never allow the pure technologist, the materialist, and the rivalry between the exact sciences to dictate the fate of humankind. Humankind must be guided by universal minds which are close to the secrets of the transcendental and which are able to bring to the Cosmic Scales of Balance more than the mere weight of technological progress.

For the past several years we have been traveling about the world, lecturing, researching, sharing thoughts with Medicine People and metaphysical visionaries. The most consistent element that we have found among these individuals is a sense of urgency which has caused a good many men and women to quit good jobs so they may await what their Medicine tells them will be a time of great cleansing and purification.

This sense of urgency is by no means limited to younger people. Men and women in their maturity are also experiencing a soul-deep sensation, which many describe as though they are standing on an enormous precipice, preparatory to leaping forward into free flight.

When we shuffle these impressions together and sort out their varying impulses, we find that these people are tuning in to an approaching major change which is about to transform society into something other than it presently encompasses.

We may be living in the most important time in all history. Recently, American Indian Medicine Priests and Shamans have been speaking out as never before. Information that has been very sacred and passed only from Medicine Priest to Medicine Priest is now being urgently shared with all who will listen, all who will treat the information with respect—and, hopefully, act upon it. This long-held secret information has to do with a Universal Plan of devastating earthquakes, famine, floods, and other major changes in our environment that will "shake us awake."

For the last ten years, the Shamans have been attempting to warn people of errant ways, to teach a path of harmony and a way of walking softly in balance on the Earth Mother. It has been the prayer and hope of the Medicine priests that the warnings and catastrophes that they have foreseen could be avoided altogether, or at least lessened, if humankind would listen and change its ways and begin to care for one another and for all living creatures of the earth, land, sea and sky.

Many have listened and are heeding the admonitions. Many others have not, and it appears that Terra will not much longer be "firma." The Earth Mother is severely out of balance and needs a major cleansing.

Over the years, we, the authors and editors of this book, have each been entrusted with information regarding American Indian prophecies and Earth changes by such powerful Medicine Priests as Sun Bear, Rolling Thunder, Grandfather David, Twylah, Kuichy and many others. Although the Shamans are doing all possible to send the message loud and clear, it still gets distorted or misunderstood. They say it is imperative that the prophetic messages are told correctly!

Our own visions tell us that this coming time of great Earth changes will not herald the end of the world, but will mark another in a series of transitional periods which are necessary for humankind's spiritual evolution. That point made, however, it is going to be a heavy time coming down on us!

The traditional Medicine Person views the Earth Mother as a relation, as an entity possessed of a nervous system, just like a human body. When the nervous system of this planet becomes upset, it has to readjust itself, just like any other organism, to get its balance. One does not have to be too astute in our day of air pollution, diminishing rain forests, nuclear radiation, and threats of global warming to recognize how humankind has upset both the ecological and spiritual balance of this planet since the last Great Cleansing occurred, probably 20,000 years ago.

Yes, there is no denying that the approaching event will be an awful one, for when the Earth Mother purges herself, there will be catastrophes on its surface; and a whole lot of people—the just and the unjust —are going to go under.

But our visions have told us that the physical cataclysms attendant with this transitional period of cleansing will be as nothing compared to the psychological cataclysms which will be experienced by those men and women who have not prepared themselves for the coming changes in societal transformation and the advent of higher consciousness. For those people who will not release their hold on material reality, we fear mass suicides and incredible epidemics of nervous breakdowns. As each month passes, we feel that it becomes increasingly imperative that we, by our books, our seminars, and—it is to be hoped—our example, alert as many of our brothers and sisters as possible to the ever-expanding, ever-widening cracks in the world of material reality.

How do we prepare for the Great Cleansing?

On the physical level, many Medicine prophets have said that we should begin storing food and water and—most important—set about regaining our balance with the Earth Mother.

On the spiritual level, as Dallas Chief Eagle of the Teton Sioux phrased it, we are going to have to cleanse ourselves by getting rid of past concepts of materialism and negativity and by coming to harmony with the Earth Mother.

Can we avoid the Great Cleansing?

Medicine traditionalists, such as Sun Bear, say that the purgative event has already happened in the Spirit World. Soon spirit time will become our time, the great Chippewa Medicine Priest, founder of the Bear Tribe, declares. There is nothing man can do to stop it.

But as Sun Bear and other visionaries see it, good people of spiritual awareness will build a better world after the cleansing has occurred. Many prophets have foreseen a spiritual and a material renaissance which will follow the great purification.

Grandmother Twylah, Repositor of Wisdom for the Seneca, has been granted a vision in which she perceived the true Medicine people have always been together, evolving through many forms of former lives along the same level of development guided by the teachers of spiritual wisdom. "Medicine people cling as one by our devotion that links us to the Creator," she has said.

Medicine people who are of the Great Light have come to walk the pathway again in order to be of service during the great cleansing of Mother Earth.

"Medicine people will seed the decrees of the Creator into the next world after the cleansing of the Earth Mother," Twylah said. "When the final transition occurs, our spiritual light will guide and protect us. Some Medicine people will evolve as people of wisdom, some will be teachers, but many of us will carry on the duties of messengers."

What of specific Earth changes during the Great Cleansing?

A few years ago, the well-known Cherokee/Shoshone Medicine Priest Rolling Thunder said that seventeen volcanoes would erupt, starting with Mr. St. Helens [and it did soon after]. Rolling Thunder is in demand both as a lecturer and a Medicine Priest because of the amazing powers that he exhibits over the elements, abilities which have been examined and documented by such august institutions as The Menninger Clinic.

Sun Bear has named very precise geographical worldwide locations which will experience earthquakes, floods, and famine. Many Medicine Priests speak of World War III.

When we were in Peru, Kuichy, a South American Shaman shared prophecies nearly identical in content with his North American Medicine brothers and sisters. The Hopis, considered the keepers of the American Indian prophecy, echo the same warnings.

Many Medicine Priests are receiving very specific things involving the coming events, "The Great Cleansing," and approximately when and where the most dramatic changes will occur. Concerned Shamans are issuing statements about what can be done about the "Purification" in terms of preparation and surviving.

Among the prophecies of forthcoming physical changes during the time of the

Great Cleansing are the following:

In the years from 1991 to 2000:

Major earthquakes will rock both the East and West coasts of the United States.

There will be a major submergence of land in the Great Lakes area, with portions of Wisconsin, Michigan, and Illinois going under water.

Land will rise in the North Sea.

Parts of the British Isles will submerge.

The Atlantic will "lap" at London's door. Off the coast of Great Britain, small land masses will arise.

Major quakes will strike China, causing lakes to form west of Peking.

As the white Medicine Priest Edgar Cayce predicted, the area around Virginia Beach will remain stable and safe. Parts of Ohio, Indiana, Illinois, and the Southern part of Canada will also remain firm.

South America will be rocked by severe earthquakes.

Large sections of Japan will be claimed by the Pacific.

Krakatoa will erupt once again.

Most of the Hawaiian Islands will sink beneath the ocean.

The year 2000 may see a pole shift in which the Earth Mother will change her axis of rotation suddenly, tumbling "head over heels." The North and South poles will be dramatically shifted to new positions, and very different climactic conditions will be established.

By the year 2030, there will be a new emphasis on the planet's various governments seeking to help people develop self-reliance and self-awareness, rather than striving to regulate personal behavior and thought. Men and women of higher consciousness will find ways to incorporate the nurturing aspects of tribal life into large scale applications. Conditions will continue to develop which will blossom into a New World of oneness and love for all facets of the Great Mystery.

We can only pray that millions of men and women will come to heed the warnings of the Great Cleansing that are being sounded by Medicine Priests through the world. We ask the God-Force, the Great Mystery, to permit us continued existence in the circle of life so that we may all live together in unity, equality, and love.

Portfolio of Amerindians

ONE: Chippewa eagle-feather headdress, embellished with deerskin trimmed in lynx, *circa,* late 1800s.

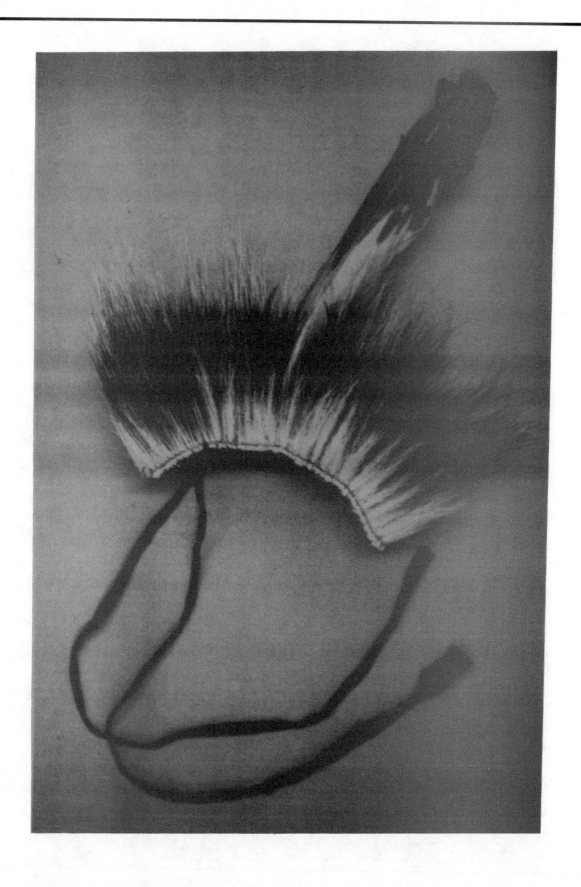

TWO: Winnebago dance roach, *circa*, late 1800s.

THREE: Actor Tom Laughlin created a new legendary Indian hero with his portrayal of Billy Jack on the screen. Laughlin had his faith in the Shawnee Medicine priest Rolling Thunder to support his courage during the filming of the rattlesnake ceremony for the motion picture *Billy Jack*.

FOUR: Legends of the Star People may be found etched in rock throughout the United States. Medicine people recorded a permanent account of the visitors from the stars in petroglyphs (rock drawings).

FIVE: Dallas Chief Eagle was made a chief of the Teton Sioux during a ceremony overseen by two descendants of the great chief Red Cloud. Now deceased, he was the author of *Winter Count* a novel rich in authentic detail of Amerindian life before the tragic massacre at Wounded Knee.

SIX: Chief Eagle served as an effective ambassador for his people during many junkets overseas. He was a marvelous storyteller who had a wealth of tales about the old ways and the myths and legends of the Plains Indians.

SEVEN: Iron Eyes Cody (left) has appeared in countless motion pictures depicting Amerindian life. He is famous for his portrayal of the "Indian with the tear" in the anti-pollution public service announcement on television. Although he considered many of his film portrayals denigrative to his people, he did perform the sacred song *Wakan Tanka* [The Great Mystery] in an authentic manner for the motion picture *A Man Called Horse*. Iron Eyes is a member of the Sioux *Yuwipi* Society, and he is very serious about his practice of the Medicine traditions. He is pictured here with the powerful Medicine priest John Fire Lame Deer, subject of the book *Lame Deer: Seeker of Visions*.

EIGHT: The site of this mass Indian burial ground in Connecticut has caused many visitors to complain of feelings of nausea. Psychic sensitives feel strong vibrations emanating from the area, and residents have long reported manifestations of Amerindian ghosts, mysterious fires, and other phenomena. The immediate area is noted for numerous apparitions of Indians, the sounds of drums, and other strange occurrences. *Credit: Gordon Alexander.*

NINE: Sun Bear, an influential Chippewa Medicine priest, is the founder of the Bear Tribe, the first new Indian tribe in this century. Sun Bear's Medicine is for both Indian and non-Indian, and much of his teachings are built around the visions which he receives.

TEN: Twylah Nitsch is the granddaughter of Moses Shongo, the last great Seneca Medicine man. Well-tutored in the traditional teachings of her people, Twylah shares with others through lectures and courses in Seneca Wisdom. Here Twylah holds the youngest member of the tribe present when Brad Steiger was adopted into the Wolf Clan of the Senecas. The baby represented new life, while a tribal elder symbolized the old, during the ceremony.

ELEVEN: Twylah with her mother, Maude Shongo Hurd.

TWELVE: Traditional Indians pray standing upright, arms outstretched. *Painting by Ernie Smith, Seneca.*

THIRTEEN: Brad Steiger stands in the tomb of a great Incan chief in the sacred city of Machupiccu, high in the mountains of the Peruvian Andes. *Photo by Sherry Hansen Steiger.*

FOURTEEN: Sherry Hansen Steiger goes into deep meditation at a sacred vortex area in Sedona, Arizona. Sherry, who is of Chippewa-Swedish heritage, is an ordained Protestant minister who also practices Medicine ways. An exceptionally deep meditator, Sherry regularly fasts and spends hours in prayer and vision-seeking in her sweat lodge.